F-15C EAGLE VS MiG-23/25

Iraq 1991

DOUGLAS C. DILDY AND TOM COOPER

First published in Great Britain in 2016 by Osprey Publishing
PO Box 883, Oxford, OX1 9PL, UK
PO Box 3985, New York, NY 10185-3985, USA
E-mail: **info@ospreypublishing.com**
Osprey Publishing, part of Bloomsbury Publishing Plc

A CIP catalogue record for this book is available from the British Library

ISBN: 978 1 4728 1270 4
PDF ISBN: 978 1 4728 1271 1
ePub ISBN: 978 1 4728 1272 8

Edited by Tony Holmes
Cover artwork and battlescene by Gareth Hector
Three-views, cockpits, armament scrap views and Engaging the Enemy artwork by Jim Laurier
Index by Mark Swift
Typeset in ITC Conduit and Adobe Garamond
Maps and tactical formation diagrams by bounford.com
Originated by PDQ Media, Bungay UK
Printed in China through World Print Ltd

16 17 18 19 20 10 9 8 7 6 5 4 3 2 1

F-15C Eagle cover art

At noon on January 19, 1991 Capt Rick "Kluso" Tollini and his wingman engaged two Iraqi Air Force (IrAF) MiG-25 "Foxbats" at low altitude above an undercast over the western Iraqi desert. Tollini engaged the "Foxbat" leader, shooting one AIM-7, whose rocket motor failed to fire, and an AIM-9 at the MiG. "The AIM-9 flew close to his [after]burner cans – through the plume and appeared to fuze – but too far aft, resulting in a miss," Tollini later recalled. "I then shot a second AIM-7. After a short pause for the launch/motor fire sequence, I saw the Sparrow missile fly out in front of my jet and begin a constant acceleration in a smooth right-hand turn that almost exactly matched the 'Foxbat's' own flightpath. Finally, I saw the missile disappear under the belly. In what seemed to take an eternity, to the point where I again considered making a gun attack, I waited for the warhead to go off. In retrospect, it appeared that the AIM-7 actually impacted the underside of the 'Foxbat', with the back-up contact fuze finally setting off the Sparrow's large blast-frag warhead. The explosion was huge, like the 'Death Star' from the *Star Wars* film! Unlike the first 'Foxbat', this one totally disintegrated in a breathtaking flash."

MiG-25 cover art

During the early hours of January 17, 1991, following an inconclusive engagement with the leader of the F/A-18C Hornets, IrAF "Foxbat" pilot Capt Zuhair Dawoud rolled out eastbound and retarded his throttles out of afterburner. Less than 20 miles off his nose, headed north, was another of the squadron's Hornets – flown by Lt Cdr Scott "Spike" Speicher – accelerating in full afterburner in preparation for a HARM launch. Dawoud later reported, "I locked a target 38km [20.5 miles] from me and at 29km [15.6 miles] I fired [the] R-40D missile. . . I kept the target locked with my radar [un]till I witnessed a huge explosion in front of me. I kept looking for the aircraft going down spirally to the ground with fire engulfing it."

Acknowledgments

Any attempt to accurately and objectively reconstruct and describe the aerial engagements in a war fought 25 years ago requires the contribution of numerous individuals, many of whom participated in the events described. Foremost, the authors thank the veterans of Operation *Desert Storm* not only for their service and efforts during that conflict, but also for their generous and considerate contributions to this book. From the USAF the authors thank Brig Gen (Ret.) Tony Schiavi and Cols (Ret.) Rick Tollini, Larry Pitts, Cesar Rodriguez, Jay Denney, Dean Powell, and Bob Hehemann for their personal accounts of their combat experiences. Helping the authors decipher, understand, and relate US Navy operations were Adm (Ret.) Mark Fitzgerald, Rear Adm (Ret.) Bob Besal and Capts (Ret.) John R. Stevenson and Bob Stumpf, Cdr (Ret.) Val Diers, and Dave "Hey Joe" Parsons. From the Iraqi side, the authors are indebted to Brig Gen (Ret.) Ahmad Sadik and researchers Ali Tobchi and Mohammed Hassan for their selfless contributions.

The ground work for this comparative study was laid by noted aviation journalist Steve Davies through his many taped interviews with participants and his contribution of numerous photographs, as well as his helpful suggestions and advice. Additionally, Craig "Quizmo" Brown paved the way with his comprehensive collection of pilot/participant interviews contained in his excellent *Debrief: A Complete History of US Aerial Engagements 1981 to the Present* (Schiffer Military History, 2007), and we appreciate his permission to use portions of some of them. We also thank fellow Osprey author Paul Crickmore and fellow (retired) F-15 pilot Bill Kurey for their insightful critiques of the manuscript. With the benefit of all these individuals' assistance – and more – we look forward to completing a similar comparative study of the F-15C Eagle versus the MiG-29 "Fulcrum" in the Duel series.

CONTENTS

INTRODUCTION

The concept of an air superiority fighter is one that is designed to fly into contested (usually enemy) airspace and have the sensors and weapons to effectively eliminate adversary fighters/interceptors, thus establishing a permissive environment for various other (typically bomb-dropping) aircraft to perform their missions without interference. In the USA, this concept was pioneered by the legendary North American Aviation (NAA) P-51 Mustang, which regularly flew from airfields in England to defeat the Luftwaffe over Berlin. Five years later, the concept was advanced and developed to near-perfection with the NAA F-86 Sabre, which, even with an early model "gas-guzzling" turbojet, flew 300 miles into "MiG Alley" and eventually dominated the Soviets' MiG-15s flying over northern Korea from neighboring Manchuria (see *Osprey Duel 50 – F-86 Sabre vs MiG-15, Korea 1950-53*).

By the time the US Air Force (USAF) next went to war – in Vietnam, beginning in earnest in 1965 – the advent of nuclear weapons and the American penchant for sophistication over specialization resulted in the USAF's fighter mainstay being the "multi-role" McDonnell Douglas F-4 Phantom II that could (so it was thought by the service's civilian overlords in the Kennedy/Johnson Administrations) defend itself getting to and from its targets, theoretically obviating the need for dedicated air superiority fighters.

During Operation *Rolling Thunder* (March 2, 1965 to April 1, 1968), strike packages being sent into North Vietnam were composed largely of Republic F-105 Thunderchiefs – a supersonic nuclear delivery platform that was forced to become a conventional fighter-bomber – with one or two four-ships of Phantom IIs (also carrying bombs) escorting them to their targets. If the MiG-17s and MiG-21s of the Vietnamese People's Air Force (VPAF) made an appearance, the Phantom II crews were to jettison their bombs and engage them. If they didn't, the F-4s would drop their bombs on (usually around) the target.

Inherited from the US Navy during a fit of politically coerced "jointness," the Phantom II was a bomber interceptor/fleet defender unsuited to the USAF's traditional air superiority mission. Compared with the products of the Mikoyan and Gurevich (MiG) design bureau, the F-4 was large and heavy. Its engines smoked when not in afterburner and consumed its fuel at alarming rates when they were, its radar was longer-ranged but could not see targets below its own altitude, its longer-ranged missiles were hobbled by visual identification (VID) requirements and it had no gun for close-in combat. But most of all, the F-4 lacked the maneuverability needed to deal effectively with the more nimble MiGs. Relative to the MiG-17, MiG-19, and MiG-21, the powerful, yet heavy, Phantom II lacked the agility needed to bring weapons to bear in a classic turning dogfight.

Consequently, the F-4 would not achieve even half of the F-86's excellent 7-to-1 Korean War record. Indeed, during *Rolling Thunder*, its kill ratio was only 3.36-to-1. Worse, the Phantom II proved unable to protect the strike packages and other air operations from MiG attack – 27 USAF aircraft (in addition to 18 F-4s) were lost to MiGs during this period. Directed by canny Ground Control Intercept (GCI) controllers, the MiG pilots usually "hid in the weeds" below the F-4's "radar horizon" and executed timely "pop up attacks" that, as a minimum, resulted in the strikers jettisoning their bomb-loads to defend themselves.

Even before the first Phantom IIs were committed to combat over North Vietnam, some fighter pilots at HQ USAF (the "Air Staff") recognized the doctrinal aberration being foisted upon their service. In February 1965, Lt Col John W. Bohn Jr wrote a position paper arguing for a "high-low mix" tactical air force, where a few dedicated high performance (and high-tech) air-to-air fighters – placing emphasis on maneuverability instead of speed – would achieve aerial superiority, allowing a host of "low tech" (and low-cost) fighter-bombers to fulfill their missions with impunity. The position was endorsed by Gen John P. McConnell, Chief of Staff USAF, and $10M was allocated for further studies leading to the design of the "ultimate dogfighter."

Two-and-a-half years later, in July 1967, the Soviets unveiling their newest fighter – a massive twin-jet, twin-tail interceptor with singularly stunning performance – suddenly gave rise to a renewed, urgent, and increased impetus to the USAF's development of an F-4 replacement. It had to have a fighter able to beat what would become known as the MiG-25 "Foxbat." For clarity and consistency, NATO Air Standards Coordinating Committee (ASCC) aircraft reporting names (sometimes called "codewords") are used throughout this work.

Unlike the Americans, following the Korean War the Soviets turned to specialization instead of sophistication. Once the development of the MiG-15/-17/-19 series had run its course, the *Protivo Vozdushnaya Oborona Strany* ("Anti-Air Defense of the Nation" or PVO-Strany – the national air defense force) expressed the need for a fast-reacting, quick-climbing, missile-armed point-defense interceptor to prevent USAF Strategic Air Command (SAC) B-52 Stratofortresses from immolating Russian cities with hydrogen bombs. The end result was the MiG-21 "Fishbed." In the confined air space of North Vietnam, the fast, nimble "Fishbed" proved its mettle against bomb-laden formations of Thunderchiefs and Phantom IIs.

Shortly afterwards, the leadership of the Soviet Union's "other air force," the *Voyenno-Vozdushnye Sily* (literally "Military Air Forces" or V-VS, which included the Soviet Union's tactical air force, known as *Frontovaya Aviahsiya* or "Frontal Aviation") focused on preventing North Atlantic Treaty Organization (NATO) fighter-bombers from neutralizing Warsaw Pact ground forces and airfields with tactical nuclear weapons. The primary threat, at the time, was the F-105, whose blazing low-altitude speed gave it great potential for penetrating current Soviet air defense systems by minimizing detection ranges, avoiding surface-to-air missiles (SAMs) and outrunning the V-VS's current stable of interceptors.

In 1960, when the USAF issued Specific Operational Requirement (SOR) 183 for the development of the "swing-wing" Tactical Fighter Experimental (TFX), this unfavorable situation promised to become dramatically problematic. The V-VS wanted the MiG-23 "Flogger" to meet and defeat the threat posed by this advanced high-speed/low-altitude penetrator.

Meanwhile, complicating the Soviet Union's strategic air defense problem was the NAA XB-70 Valkyrie, the developmental contract for which had been issued on January 24, 1958. Driven by six huge afterburning turbojets, the XB-70 was capable of reaching Mach 3.2 while flying at 70,000ft (21,000m) – speeds and altitudes that would easily evade the current crop of Soviet interceptor aircraft, and made it untouchable by the SAMs then in service. While technological advances in the latter ultimately resulted in the program's demise, PVO-Strany initiated the development of a specific interceptor to meet and destroy the high-speed/high-altitude penetrator, resulting in the MiG-25 "Foxbat." While, at the time, American intelligence services had no real knowledge of what would become the "Flogger" (because even the Russians were unsure at that stage), the unveiling of the MiG-25 sent shock waves through the upper echelons of the USAF's leadership. Indeed, it prompted an urgent reissue of the formal Request for Proposal (RFP – the first, issued in December 1965 for a general "Tactical Support Aircraft," had indifferent responses) calling for development of an air-to-air "Fighter" with the performance to beat the MiG-25. In its developmental period, since the numerical designation could not yet be known, the design would be called the "F-X".

A McDonnell Douglas F-15C of the 433rd Fighter Weapons School pulls away from its tanker before beginning its role in a Red Flag "Large Force Employment Exercise". Not only was the Eagle designed to be technically superior to all other fighters of its day, but the USAF's constant and intense training programs – especially those flown over the Nevada desert environment – forged in its pilots the proficiency needed to beat any of them. (USAF)

CHRONOLOGY

1961

February 16 Secretary of Defense (SecDef) Robert McNamara directs the USAF and US Navy to develop a single aircraft to satisfy the requirements for both the USAF's tactical strike mission and the US Navy's fleet air defense mission, giving birth to the ill-fated, joint-service Tactical Fighter Experimental (TFX) program.

March 10 Mikoyan OKB is directed to design a high-altitude supersonic aircraft to fulfill the requirements for a PVO strategic interceptor and V-VS reconnaissance aircraft, work commencing on the Ye-155 project.

1963

December 3 MiG OKB directed to begin development of a new tactical fighter incorporating the S-23 weapons system.

1964

March 6 First flight of the MiG-25 reconnaissance version prototype, Ye-155R.

September 9 First flight of the MiG-25 interceptor version prototype, Ye-155P.

September 21 First flight of the North American XB-70 supersonic high-altitude nuclear bomber.

December 21 First flight of the General Dynamics F-111A, fulfilling the USAF's TFX requirement.

1965

March 16 MiG's Ye-155 prototypes begin setting 29 speed, altitude, and time-to-climb records – seven of them are absolute world records.

March 1965 to April 1968 Over North Vietnam, Operation *Rolling Thunder* proves the inadequacy of not having a dedicated air superiority fighter in the USAF inventory.

April 29 HQ USAF initiates the F-X program.

"Red 45", a fully armed MiG-25PD "Foxbat-E" (the PVO Strany's iconic Cold War strategic interceptor), in flight alongside a US Navy intelligence/reconnaissance platform. (DVIC)

November State acceptance trials for MiG-25 begin.

December 8 USAF issues the first RFP to US aerospace manufacturers, soliciting proposals for the F-X.

1967

June 10 First flight of the MiG-23 prototype.

July 9 At Domodedovo airshow, among 12 new aircraft types debuted is the first MiG-23 and four MiG-25 prototypes, stunning Western observers.

August 12 USAF issues its second RFP, requiring the design of an air superiority fighter with performance superior to "any present or projected Soviet-designed fighter."

1968

July SecDef Clark Clifford stops work on US Navy F-111B. US Navy pursues development of the Grumman F-14 Tomcat as its Fleet Air Defense fighter, leaving the USAF free to pursue its own follow-on fighter aircraft, the F-X.

September Secretary of the Air Force (SecAF) Harold Brown signs HQ USAF Development Concept Paper (DCP) establishing the technical and performance requirements for the F-X.

September 30 USAF issues third F-X-related RFP, requiring respondents' proposals to meet the requirements detailed in SecAF's DCP.

1969

May First operational MiG-23s begin V-VS service trials.

Summer First operational MiG-25s begin PVO service trials.

December 23 USAF selects McDonnell Douglas as prime contractor for development and production of the F-15.

1970

April 28 MiG-25P State acceptance and service trials complete, the interceptor is cleared for full-scale production and service entry.

The MiG-23M "Flogger-B" was built specifically as a tactical fighter for the V-VS, this particular example being shown in flight with two R-23 medium-range missiles and a pair of R-60 short-range "dogfight" missiles. (DVIC)

1972

June	First flight of the MiG-23M "Flogger-B."
July 27	First flight of the McDonnell Douglas F-15A Eagle.

1973

June 4 – July 25	MiG-25 prototypes break/establish four new time-to-climb records to altitudes of and above 20,000m.

1974

Summer	First deliveries of the MiG-23MS made to Iraq.

1975

February 1	F-15A 72-0119 "Streak Eagle" completes sweep of all eight FAI time-to-climb records.
September	First F-15A squadron declared operationally ready.

1976

September 6	Lt V. I. Belenko defects to the USA, flying MiG-25P "Red 31" to Hakodate, Japan, compromising the aircraft, radar, and IFF systems.

1977

June	First flight of the improved MiG-23ML "Flogger-G."

1978

Spring	MiG-25PD "Foxbat-E" successfully completes its State acceptance trials and is ordered into production. All existing MiG-25Ps ordered upgraded to PDS standard.

1979

February 26	First flight of the improved F-15C Eagle.
July 16	Saddam Hussein, General Secretary of the Iraqi Ba'ath Party (an Arab nationalism/socialism mix), becomes President of Iraq.
Summer	First deliveries of MiG-25s made to Iraq.

1980

September 22	Saddam Hussein launches full-scale invasion of Iran, beginning the Iraq–Iran War.

1988

August 20	UN Resolution 598 finally ends combat operations between Iran and Iraq.

1989

December	Following a series of USA–USSR Summits, negotiations, nuclear weapons treaties, and other agreements, President Bush and Prime Minister Gorbachev officially declare the Cold War "over" during the Malta Summit.

1990

August 2	Saddam Hussein occupies Kuwait. IrAF MiG-25RBs begin flying reconnaissance missions along Saudi Arabian border.
August 7	First USAF unit – F-15Cs of the 71st TFS – deploys to Saudi Arabia for Operation *Desert Shield.*

1991

January 17	Operation *Desert Storm* begins.
January 19	First combat between USAF F-15Cs and IrAF MiG-25s.
January 23	Lt Gen Chuck Horner announces CENTAF has achieved air superiority over Iraq.
January 26	Evacuation of IrAF combat aircraft to Iran begins.
January 30	Final combat between USAF F-15Cs and IrAF MiG-25s.
February 24	Coalition forces launch ground offensive to liberate Kuwait.
February 28	Ceasefire goes into effect, ending full-scale hostilities in Iraq.

DESIGN AND DEVELOPMENT

MiG-23 "FLOGGER"

The story of the development of the MiG-23 "Flogger" is that of a weapons system looking for an airplane. Through several technical bureaus the V-VS had sought to develop an effective air intercept (AI) radar coupled with reliable medium-range air-to-air missiles. Recognizing the limitations imposed by radar's "ground clutter" when looking down from the aircraft's altitude or when operating at low level, the service also sought an effective infra-red (IR) sensor able to detect the "heat signature" of the afterburning turbojets powering Western aircraft (mostly USAF F-4s, F-105s, and F-111s) that were capable of carrying tactical nuclear weapons. Anticipating incorporating all of these systems in the next generation fighter from the MiG design bureau (*Opytno-Konstrooktorskoye Byuro*, or OKB), the V-VS designated the sensors/weapons suite the S-23, after the new "Sapfir-23" (Sapphire-23) AI radar. On December 3, 1963, the MiG OKB was instructed to begin development of a new tactical fighter incorporating the S-23 weapons system.

The OKB's first obstacle was mating the large Sapfir-23 radar to an airframe – a problem because the MiG designers had previously used open nose intakes to supply air directly to the aircraft's jet engine(s). In earlier designs radars had been afterthoughts "scabbed" onto either the upper lip or the splitter of the intake (as in the MiG-17P/

PF and MiG-19P) or mounted within the central, moveable supersonic "spike" (on the MiG-21). The sheer size of the Sapfir precluded either of these options. The whole nose had to be devoted to the radar, other sensors, and associated electronics, meaning that the air intakes would have to be applied to the fuselage. The MiG designers opted for side intakes by copying directly from the Lockheed F-104 Starfighter.

Izdeliye 23-01 "Blue 23" makes an impressively short takeoff at the Moscow-Domodedovo airshow in July 1967. (Foxbat Files)

As this technical challenge was being overcome the V-VS threw the OKB a "curve ball" by insisting, in 1964, that the type include a Short Takeoff and Landing (STOL) capability. Concerned that NATO tactical nuclear weapons would render the Warsaw Pact's large peacetime air bases unusable in any future European conflict, the V-VS planned to disperse its fighters to short, primitive, camouflaged "campaign fields." To launch from such austere locations STOL capability was required, and the MiG bureau undertook two independent but parallel courses of study – lift-engines and variable geometry (VG) wings – to develop a solution to this new and drastically complicating requirement.

Under engineer A. Andreyev, *Izdeliye 23-01* ("Article 23-01") would investigate incorporating two Kolesov R36-35 turbojet lift-engines into a new fighter airframe. This prototype flew on April 3, 1967 and demonstrated its impressive STOL performance at the Moscow-Domodedovo airshow. Just in case it showed up in the V-VS inventory, NATO's ASCC dubbed it the "Faithless."

Former test pilot Grigoriy A. Sedov led the design team for *Izdeliye 23-11*, investigating the STOL potential of a VG configuration. Fortunately, Sedov's team had the benefit of General Dynamics' highly publicized F-111 "swing wing" design and the MMKB (*Moskovskoe Machinostroitel'noye KB* or Moscow Mechanical

Izdeliye 23-11/1 "Blue 231" was the first MiG-23 variable geometry wing prototype, and it is seen here with its wings fully swept back and notional R-23 missiles mounted beneath the wing gloves. (Foxbat Files)

V-VS MiG-23ML "Flogger-G" "Red 21" was photographed during a deployment to Finland in August 1978. (Authors' Collection)

Engineering Design Bureau) was able to replicate an almost identical structure, including using the same 16-degree, 45-degree and 72-degree wing sweep positions. Similarly, the F-4's two-dimensional (rectangular cross-section) air intakes were copied, replacing the F-104-style intakes.

The first MiG-23 prototype (*Izdeliye 23-11/1*) flew on June 10, 1967 and it, too, was demonstrated at the Domodedovo airshow. By this point the VG version was selected and Mikoyan was authorized to construct three developmental prototypes and six pre-production examples. Factory trials and State acceptance tests were completed by July of the following next year.

The development of the S-23's complicated sensor/weapons suite lagged behind airframe design, coming along in bits and pieces. As a complete system it would consist of Sapfir-23 AI radar, the TP-23 infrared search and track sensor (IRSTS), and the ASP-23 automatic computing gunsight, all supporting the K-23 medium-range air-to-air and Kh-23 air-to-surface missiles. However, when series production of the initial batch of 50 aircraft began in May 1969 at the *Moskovskiy Mashinostroitel'nyy Zavod* ("Moscow Machinery Plant") No. 30, only five were completed with the intended radar and none had the TP-23.

The initial batch was issued to the Lipetsk test flight facility and the V-VS's 116th *Istrebitelniy Aviatsionniy Polk* (IAP, "Fighter Aviation Regiment") in Belarus for service tests. The aircraft quickly became a huge disappointment to test and fighter pilots alike. Accustomed as they were to the near-viceless flying qualities of the MiG-21, the OKB's latest product had tricky handling characteristics, inherent lack of maneuverability, and a restrictive 5.55G turning limitation. Worse, it was accident prone – resulting in two complete redesigns of the wings – and the Sapfir-23 proved chronically unreliable, requiring two developmental iterations to become operational. Consequently, service trials were excruciatingly protracted (four years), during which time only another 90–120 examples were produced because of the fits and starts caused by trying to incorporate major design changes while aircraft were moving down the assembly line.

Not surprisingly, the first true production version of the "Flogger" was known as the MiG-23M (for *Modifitseerovannyy* or "modified"), first flown in June 1972. It mounted the S-23D-III (D for *Dorabotannyy* or "improvement" and III for "number three") fire control system that mated the Sapfir-23D (NATO codename "High Lark") to the AVM-23 analog computer to recognize and reduce "ground clutter" and present the processed data on the ASP-23 gunsight's combining glass. Guiding the Vympel R-23R (NATO designated AA-7A "Apex"), which was finally fielded in 1974, the S-23D-III system at last gave the V-VS its first beyond-visual-range (BVR) and front aspect engagement capabilities.

Powered by the uprated 18,300lb thrust (27,563lb in afterburner) Khachaturov R29-300, the "Flogger-B" was an extremely fast interceptor, although it remained tricky to fly and was handicapped by poor maneuverability. While structurally strengthened to sustain 8G with the wings at the 45-degree setting, its capricious aerodynamics made it prone to sudden, untelegraphed, and violent departures from controlled flight, frequently before the G-limit was reached.

In an effort to enhance the handling and maneuverability, in January 1975 MiG OKB flew the improved "Flogger-G," produced for the V-VS as the MiG-23ML (L for *Lyohkiy* or "lightweight") and as the PVO-Strany's MiG-23P (for *Perekhvatchik* or "interceptor"). The structural improvements and the new, lighter, more compact Sapfir-23ML radar resulted in a 1,450lb (660kg) weight saving, while strengthening some parts of the airframe raised the G-limit to 8.5Gs with 45-degree wing sweep. However, leading edge extensions on the wings and aerodynamic changes to the wing glove did not cure its erratic and vicious handling deficiencies.

MiG-25 "FOXBAT"

The design concept that resulted in the MiG-25 originated at the 1959 Paris airshow, where Artyom I. Mikoyan got a close look at the brand-new (maiden flight on August 3, 1958) NAA A5J Vigilante – the US Navy's large, carrier-based nuclear-strike attack jet. An all-new "layout" was warranted because MiG's latest designs, the Ye-150 and Ye-152 ("Ye" was the abbreviation for *yedinitsa* or "one-off" prototype), both looked very much like MiG-21s on steroids. They had also recently lost the competition for PVO-Strany's "heavy interceptor" requirement to the Tupolev Tu-128, a huge, long-range two-seater with a large nose to house the bulky *Radio Pritsel-Smerch* ("radio-sight [e.g. radar] Tornado" or RP-S) radar and a second cockpit for its operator.

Designed to intercept USAF B-47 and B-52 bombers at the periphery of the Soviet empire rather than allow them to get close enough to Russian cities to incinerate them, PVO leadership knew that the big "Fiddler" would have a much tougher time against the supersonic B-58 Hustler (replacing the B-47) and XB-70 Valkyrie (intended to supplant the B-52).

The problem with MiG OKB's Ye-150 and Ye-152 was that it was difficult to incorporate the (then state-of-the-art) vacuum-tube technology radars into the supersonic fighters' conical intake "spike" no matter how much the company "super-sized" the airframe. Consequently, when Mikoyan encountered systems integration engineer Ya. I. Seletskiy in the OKB corridors one day, he suggested, "draw an interceptor along the lines of the Vigilante, but powered by two R15-300 engines, designed to fly at 3,000km/hr [1,620 knots] and without the all-too-sophisticated high-lift devices [needed for delta-wing designs]."

Opposite
Painted in flat light gray overall (Soviet Colour 593, similar to FS36375), with all dielectric panels in flat dark gull gray (between FS36081 and 36099), and an anti-glare panel in flat black (FS27030), Iraqi MiG-25s were very similar in general appearance to their Soviet brethren. National markings were applied in six positions, with those on either side of the wings being canted outwards. As of 1991, their serial numbers (always applied in black below the cockpit), consisted of five digits, the first two of which denoted the type, the third the version, and the last two the individual aircraft. Correspondingly, serials of IrAF MiG-25PD/PDSs were in the range 252xx (shown here is serial number 25211, flown by Capt M. J. as-Sammarai in January 1991). All maintenance stencils and warnings around the aircraft were applied in English language.

About this time, to effectively counter the supersonic B-58 and XB-70, PVO-Strany issued the requirement for a high-speed (Mach 3), high-altitude (20,000m/65,600ft) "heavy interceptor." Concurrently, the V-VS requested a photo-reconnaissance platform of nearly identical performance. Having suggested the possibility and advantage of fulfilling both requirements by simply changing the nose, the MiG OKB was directed in February 1961 to meet both specifications with the new Ye-155 design. Preliminary work began on March 10, 1961, with Mikoyan's partner, Mikhail I. Gurevich, being responsible for the airframe and his assistant, Nikolay Z. Matyuk, overseeing weapon system development for the Ye-155P (*Perekhvatchik*/"interceptor"). However, Gurevich's failing health soon resulted in Matyuk heading both parts of the process, becoming the project chief.

Design of the aircraft was fairly straightforward – a conventional twin-engined configuration using side-mounted, wedge-profile, two-dimensional (rectangular) air intakes with, like the Vigilante, variable-position "ramps" to control the supersonic airflow. The large – both broad and long – center-section beneath the trapezoidal wings would hold a huge volume of fuel for the bulky, powerful, and voraciously thirsty Turmansky R15B-300 afterburning turbojets. The wide "back" of the aircraft was anticipated to "blank out" a single vertical tail at high angles of attack (such as in combat turns or on final approach for landing), especially in the event of an engine failure, so twin outward-angled tails were mounted instead.

During this period, aerodynamic capabilities were advancing by leaps and bounds – much faster than the concurrent, and sluggish, electronic, radar and missile technologies. Consequently, the new airplane design was initially saddled with a dated and obsolescing weapons system. Developed for the Tu-128, MiG's newest interceptor would have to use – at least until something better came along – the *RP-Smerch* (NATO reporting name "Big Nose") fire control radar, paired with the medium-range Raduga K-9M (NATO AA-4 "Awl") air-to-air missile developed for the Ye-152A "Flipper" prototype. Upgraded to the *Smerch-A* ("Tornado-A," NATO "Foxfire"), the radar's designation was later changed to RP-25.

Six months after the Ye-155R-1 (*Razvedchik-1* for "reconnaissance, first article") made its maiden flight, the Ye-155P-1 prototype took to the air on September 9, 1964. By this time some of the aircraft's adverse aerodynamic proclivities, such as

The Ye-155P-1, seen here carrying two R-40 missile mock-ups, was the first MiG-25 interceptor prototype. (Foxbat Files)

MiG-25PD "FOXBAT"

During one of several flypasts at the Moscow-Domodedovo airshow, Ye-155R-3 "Red 3155" (a MiG-25 reconnaissance prototype) is escorted by a Ye-155P interceptor prototype – one of the two to be built. (Foxbat Files)

uncommanded – and unstoppable – roll while accelerating through Mach, had been corrected. The two Ye-155P prototypes, along with three pre-production examples, were used by the MiG OKB for "factory trials" at Ramenskoye Air Base (AB), located in Zhukovsky, while the remaining six pre-production machines were flown in the State acceptance trials conducted by the *Nauchno-Issledovatelyskii Institut* (the Air Force "Scientific and Research Institute" or NII) at Akhtubinsk, in southern Russia.

Within a year of the design's first flight, the *Fédération Aéronautique Internationale* (FAI) received official documentation claiming that, on March 16, 1965, MiG OKB test pilot Alekxandr V. Fedotov set world speed records flying the "Ye-266 powered by two R266 turbojets." These spurious designations stemmed from the record-setting "Ye-166" (the modified Ye-152-1) powered by "R166" engines with the same thrust rating. This alerted Western intelligence services to the fact that a new MiG product, powered by two Tumansky R15B-300 turbojets, was in the flight test phase. The notifications continued to pour in to the Swiss-based FAI, which accorded the Ye-155 a total of 29 records. Seven of these were absolute world records – speed over several different-sized closed courses, altitude, and "time-to-climb" for reaching altitudes above 20,000m (65,617ft). The Ye-155 was the first aircraft ever to establish a time-to-climb record to 35,000m (114,830ft).

The large number of impressive, if not shocking, records set by MiG's latest product (using the P-1, R-1, and R-3 prototypes) created acute anxiety amongst Western intelligence services because, for another two years, there were no photographs and no information other than FAI data published about the new jet. Interest in seeing the record-breaking aircraft was at a peak when President Leonid Brezhnev's regime chose to impress the aviation world with the dramatic "50th Anniversary of the October Revolution" airshow at Moscow's Domodedovo airport. A four-ship formation – composed of the Ye-155R-3 prototype escorted by three Ye-155Ps (P-1, P-2, and P-5), all flown by NII test pilots – made a sensational flyby, followed by pairs and individual high-speed flypasts, some of them in afterburner.

"Blue 06" was an early production MiG-25P used in test work at Strigino airfield near Gorky, now Nizhny Novgorod. (Foxbat Files)

Because of the urgency created by increasing CIA A-12 and USAF SR-71 overflights, the MiG-25P (*Izdeliye 84*) entered production in 1969, even before its State trials were complete. The aircraft were manufactured by the Gorky (No. 21) aircraft factory in Nizhny Novgorod and issued to the nearby PVO-Strany regiment, which was collocated with a "fighter weapons school" (FWS) that was tasked with developing high/fast-flyer intercept profiles and combat tactics. Essentially, these were the type's "service trials," with the PVO-FWS successfully firing new Bisnovat R-40 (NATO AA-6 "Acrid") missiles at front and rear (stern attack) hemisphere/aspect targets from as high as 20,000m (65,617ft) and supersonic speeds (2,700km/hr or 1,458 knots). These included 105 missile firings at 33 different remote/radio controlled targets, from unmanned Il-28M subsonic bombers and M-21 (MiG-21 drone) fighters to relatively low-altitude KRM anti-ship cruise missiles.

State acceptance and PVO-Strany service trials were completed in late 1969, by which time some 693 test flights had been conducted. The "Act of Acceptance" (April 28, 1970) stated that the type "generally meets the requirements" of PVO-Strany as to the "practical and dynamic ceiling, maximum speed, intercept range, kill probability, G-limits, radar and missile launch ranges, [and] scramble time." The test pilots certified that "piloting techniques at subsonic speeds are quite similar to existing interceptors, except for high stick forces in pitch movement. Takeoff and landing is easy. The aircraft can be mastered by pilots with flying experience on contemporary interceptors after taking a transition course."

F-15 EAGLE

Motivated by the Foxbat's astonishing appearance at the dramatic Domodedovo airshow, little more than a month later the HQ USAF issued its second F-X RFP, this one requiring a design to beat "any present or projected Soviet-designed fighter." Six American aerospace companies responded to the RFP. Still enamored with the sophistication and "top end" performance inherent in the VG technologies, half of these – General Dynamics, Lockheed, and Grumman – offered designs featuring the "swing wing" configuration. Of the other three, Fairchild Hiller (formerly Republic) favored an engines-in-the-wings layout and NAA adopted an advanced blended wing–body concept. McDonnell Douglas offered a rather conventional twin-engined configuration with twin tails. In December 1967, the USAF chose one contender from each of the two groups, awarding contracts to General Dynamics and "McAir" for further developments of their designs, with Concept Formulation Study results being due in six months.

That gave Air Force Systems Command time to begin working with engine and radar contractors. High-bypass turbofans – the major engine development of the 1960s – promised to give the fighter great fuel economy and extended range, but high thrust-on-demand (i.e. afterburner) was needed for quick acceleration to engage and for sustaining high-G maneuvering for "the kill." RFPs were sent to General Motors, General Electric, and Pratt & Whitney in April 1968, with the latter two manufacturers being awarded initial engineering development contracts based on their responses.

Opposite
F-15C-38-MC Eagle 84-0025 was flown by Capt Jay T. "OP" Denney during the climactic MiG-23 engagement on January 27, 1991 – it is depicted here after the jet had returned to Bitburg. The only Eagle pilot to down two MiGs during Operation *Desert Storm*, Denney's AIM-9M kills also proved to be the only MiGs destroyed by Sidewinders. Having flown with the 33rd TFW from August 1986, this aircraft arrived at Bitburg AB, Germany, in December and was duly assigned to the 53rd TFS "Tigers." Following a brief stint at Spangdahlem AB, it was transferred back Stateside to the 1st FW in 1999, but returned to USAFE in October 2001 when it was assigned to the 493rd FS at RAF Lakenheath, UK. The airplane is presently serving with the 44th FS/18th Wing at Kadena AB, Okinawa.

Mating an afterburner to a turbofan was problematic, but not insurmountable.

A powerful new radar was needed that could detect small radar-cross-section targets, such as the MiG-21, at great ranges and be able to look below the fighter's altitude to find such targets against the electronic clutter of "ground returns." The solution was in the development of Doppler radars that – unlike ordinary pulse radars – measured the returning radio frequency (RF) energy for frequency compression caused by the closing speed of the target. But Doppler radars could not measure distance, so evolving computer technology was used to encode the very rapid (high pulse repetition frequency, or PRF) out-going bursts of RF energy and then time the code's return to determine the range of that particular batch of electrons. Both Hughes and Westinghouse had developed Doppler radar technology sufficiently for practical application and, in March 1968, both were issued competitive awards to provide the F-X with a useable, long-range, look-down radar.

As the responses from the various contractors were finalized and submitted during the summer, the Air Staff – working closely with Tactical Air Command (TAC), which would evaluate and initially field the new fighter – now knew what was realistically possible in airframe, engine, and radar technologies. It duly drafted the F-X Development Concept Paper (DCP), outlining the requirements for what was to become the F-15. A third RFP, written to require the contractors' submissions to meet the specifications in the DCP, was issued in September 1968, with the final three contenders being selected at the end of the year. These three – North American Rockwell, Fairchild Hiller, and McDonnell Douglas – submitted their responses six months later, and after careful evaluation, on December 23, 1969 it was announced that "McAir's" Model 199-B design would become the F-15.

The very first Eagle – F-15A-1-MC tail number 71-0280 – rolled out of McAir's Saint Louis factory on June 26, 1972, the first of 12 pre-production examples (71-0280 to -0291) built for Contractor Development Test and Evaluation in California. Shipped overnight to Edwards Air Force Base (AFB) aboard a Lockheed C-5A Galaxy, '280 – commonly known as "F-1" – made its maiden flight the next day in the hands of experienced "McAir" test pilot Irving L. Burrows. His first impressions were very favorable. "Maneuvering qualities are in excess of anything ordered by the customer," he wrote. "It's a genuine pleasure to suck the Eagle into a turn that leaves any chase airplane staggering around unable to hold either the G or the speed."

After 30 months and 2,700 flying hours of contractor testing, and overcoming most of the difficulties presented by the powerful, yet temperamental, Pratt & Whitney F100-PW-100 afterburning turbofan, six of the "prototypes" were joined by eight other pre-production aircraft (72-0113 to -0120) for the Air Force Developmental Testing and Evaluation. TAC's Follow-on Operational Testing and Evaluation began in March 1975 at Luke AFB, Arizona, using six production F-15As (selected from the 73-0085/-0114 batch) and the first TF-15A two-seaters. The rest of this initial batch was delivered to the 58th Tactical Training Wing, which formed the type's Replacement Training Unit (RTU) – the first squadron being the reestablished 555th Tactical Fighter Training Squadron (TFTS), which was renowned for shooting down more MiGs (19) over North Vietnam than any other unit. The "Triple Nickel" trained its cadre of instructors, who in turn began teaching the pilots assigned to establish the first operational F-15 squadron, the 27th Tactical Fighter

F-15C EAGLE

F-15A "F-7" (71-0286), which served as the Contractor Development, Test, and Evaluation armament test bed, fires an AIM-7F Sparrow II in October 1973. (Boeing via Steve Davies)

Squadron (TFS), part of the 1st Tactical Fighter Wing (TFW), based at Langley AFB, Virginia.

While "McAir" was producing 384 F-15As and equipping five fighter wings (1st TFW at Langley AFB, Virginia; 18th TFW at Kadena AB, Okinawa; 33rd TFW at Eglin AFB, Florida; 36th TFW at Bitburg AB, Germany; and the 49th TFW at Holloman AFB, New Mexico, each with three squadrons) and an independent squadron (32nd TFS at Soesterberg RNlAFB, The Netherlands), the SPO and the design team were exploring ways to improve an already superior air-to-air fighter. By any measure, the Eagle was large for a fighter, but in it "McAir" engineers had provided significant room for growth. The F-15C took advantage of this.

The most important of these improvements was the increase in internal fuel capacity and the ability to carry conformal fuel tanks (CFTs). Internally, the two wing and main fuselage tanks were enlarged to hold a total of 25,350lbs of fuel. Additionally, the landing gear was strengthened so that a third external tank (another 3,965lbs of fuel) and CFTs could be carried while fully armed. Adding the plumbing, pneumatics, and electrical connections to carry CFTs allowed an additional 9,800lbs of fuel to be carried and gave the fully loaded Eagle an endurance of 5 hrs 20 min. This permitted the F-15C to fly 1,060 miles into contested airspace, patrol/fight for 20 minutes, and return with a 30-minute fuel reserve, all without air-to-air refueling.

The first F-15C flew on February 26, 1979, the new variant being appreciably more effective in the air-to-air role than the A-model Eagle. It would duly provide the USAF with a huge advantage over its potential adversaries, as – within 12 years – Operation *Desert Storm* was soon to show.

The F-15C prototype (78-0468) during its maiden flight, on February 26, 1979, over St Louis, Missouri. (Foxbat Files)

TECHNICAL SPECIFICATIONS

MiG-23ML "FLOGGER-G"

The Iraqi Air Force (IrAF, formally the *Al Quwwa al-Jawwiya al-Iraqiya*) received five versions of the MiG-23 from 1974 through to the late 1980s. The first to arrive were 18 extremely limited MiG-23MS interceptors ("Flogger-Es") and a few MiG-23UB ("Flogger-C") conversion trainers, all entering service with No. 39 Sqn. Although the IrAF had lost at least 12 of these in accidents by 1978, attrition was made good through further small-scale purchases. In 1982, No. 39 Sqn was re-equipped with 16 MiG-23MF "Flogger-Bs" while surviving MiG-23MSs and UBs were passed to No. 59 Operational Conversion Unit (OCU). A year later Iraq received the first of an eventual 55 MiG-23ML "Flogger-Gs," as well as at least 54 MiG-23BN "Flogger-H" ground-attack variants. Many of these were lost in the grueling eight-year Iraq–Iran War, but sufficient air defense types remained to equip three squadrons (Nos. 63, 73, and 93) at a nominal strength of 16 jets each.

Externally, the MiG-23ML *Eksportnyy* was identical to the standard V-VS "Flogger-G." Internally, the heart of the "Flogger" was the S-23MLA (A for *Ametist* or "amethyst") weapons system, consisting of the RP-23MLAE Sapfir III (N003E) J-band pulse radar paired with the newer ASP-17ML computing gunsight, enabling employment of the improved Vympel R-24R (AA-7C "Apex") semi-active radar

The MiG-23ML cockpit. Notice the lack of a radar scope and the vertical white line down the near-center of the instrument panel, which was used as a visual reference for the pilot when centering the stick during spin recovery. (Author's Collection)

(SAR) homing missile at BVR ranges.

For this version, the Sapfir had been redesigned for engaging only airborne targets in the "front quarter" (head-to-head). The radar had no capability for detecting or tracking targets it was chasing (i.e. the "rear hemisphere"). Its twist-cassegrain antenna swept the airspace ahead +/-30 degrees either side of the fighter's nose and +/- six degrees in elevation. This thin slice of airspace was dictated because the system did not include a radar scope in the cockpit. Instead, radar data was fed through the AVM-23 analog computer and presented on the large ASP-23ML combining glass, generously called a "heads-up-display" (HUD). Therefore, the vertical field-of-view (FOV) of the "HUD" constrained the elevation limitations of the Sapfir III's radar scan to fit on its combining glass.

Searching this rather confined slice of airspace, the Sapfir III could detect an approaching Tu-16 medium bomber as far away as 29.7 nautical miles (nm/55km), or 24.3nm (45km) for a MiG-21-sized target on a closing flight-path. (Because of the close similarity between radar [6,080ft] and nautical [6,076ft] miles, Western radars use nautical miles for range information, which also makes it compatible with airspeed and navigation information used in flight. All distance references in this work are in nautical miles. A nautical mile is 1.1508 statute miles.)

For closing targets at or above the "Flogger's" altitude, the radar could track ("lock-onto") a target inside 18.9nm (35km), which was approximately the maximum range of the R-24R missile when fired head-on at high altitude. To detect targets below the radar's altitude, the AVM-23 computer used an "external coherence method" to detect a target passing across/through the "clutter" caused by the earth's radar return (called "moving target indicator"). This computer process had severe limitations due to numerous "blind zones" in multiples of the radar's PRF, being able to only detect targets in the duration between successive pulses, and was limited to much shorter detection ranges (16.2nm/30km).

Operationally, because the Sapfir III searched a very thin slice of air, the MiG-23 had to be flown very close to the target's altitude, and positioned well ahead of it, for the radar to "see" it – a requirement that in turn created a critical need for accurate and timely GCI information that would position the "Flogger" at or near the target's altitude, in its "front quarter" (i.e. with closing geometry) at a range that allowed the pilot to locate and lock onto the adversary.

Because the Sapfir III was designed exclusively for front-quarter intercepts and R-24R employment, the TP-23 IRSTS was provided to allow MiG-23 pilots to engage targets in their "rear hemisphere." In a "stern chase" look-down scenario the TP-23 could locate a high-speed, afterburning (i.e. thermally "hot") target ahead and the

A Soviet "Flogger-G" carrying a full missile suite – a Vympel R-24R radar-guided missile beneath the left wing glove, a R-24T heat-seeking missile under the right wing glove and pairs of Molniya R-60MK IR "dogfight missiles" on two under-fuselage stations. Of limited use because of the MiG-23's speed and lack of maneuverability, the R-60 could, however, be employed for snap-shots against targets of opportunity. (Author's Collection)

S-23 system would "slave" the seeker head of the IR-guided R-24T, the lock-on being indicated by an aural tone in the pilot's headset. Range determination was, however, problematic and exacerbated because, in the "tail chase" mode, the R-24 had significantly reduced range, depending on the MiG's overtake airspeed.

For close-in "dogfighting" in the visual arena, the type carried two or four Molniya (now Vympel) R-60MK (NATO AA-8 "Aphid") heat-seeking missiles and was equipped with the ventrally mounted, twin-barrel Gryazev-Shipunov GSh-23L 23mm cannon with 200 rounds of ammunition, fired using the ASP-23ML's optical gunsight information. For IFF, the "Flogger-G" used the SRZO-2 transponder and had an SPO-10 Sirena-3 radar warning receiver (RWR).

Despite its sensor/weapons suite limitations, there was no denying that the MiG-23ML was a high-performance fighter. The Khachaturov R35F-300 was a powerful engine – 18,480lbs thrust in "military power" and 28,665lbs thrust in full afterburner – that could drive the "Flogger" to tremendous speeds with the "wings back." While intended for use mainly against low-altitude tactical strike aircraft, it excelled above 36,100ft (11,000m), where it could reach Mach 2.35 (approximately 1,350 knots/2,500km/h), with an astonishing rate-of-climb (42,312ft/min) and a service ceiling of more than 61,000ft (18,600m).

While excelling in sheer performance, the MiG-23 was "a handful to fly." During 1980-88, in a recently declassified program codenamed "Constant Peg," the USAF acquired ten flyable "Floggers" to investigate the new Soviet fighter's capabilities, and to "exploit" them by exposing F-14/F-15 pilots to fighting Frontal Aviation's primary air superiority aircraft. The MiGs were flown by the 4477th "Red Eagles" Test and Evaluation Squadron (TES), a unit chock full of USAF Fighter Weapons School (FWS) graduates, hand-picked "Aggressor" pilots, and US Navy Topgun instructors, based at Tonopah airfield, deep in the restricted airspace of the Nellis AFB ranges.

MiG-23ML "FLOGGER-G" ARMAMENT

The primary weapons of MiG-23MLs in service with the IrAF in 1991 were R-24R semi-active-radar-homing and R-24T infra-red-homing air-to-air missiles (ASCC-code AA-7 "Apex"). One of each variant was carried on the APU-23M1 launch rail installed under the wing-gloves, with the R-24T usually on the starboard/right-hand side. Although generally quite effective for weapons of their generation, the R-24R in particular suffered from short effective range for a missile of its size. The warhead (same on both variants) also often proved insufficient to bring down a two-engined target. Secondary armament consisted of a pair of highly maneuvrable, yet diminutive, R-60MK (ASCC-code AA-8 "Aphid") infra-red-homing, short-range air-to-air missiles. Internal armament consisted of a twin-barrelled GSh-23L 23mm automatic cannon. Powered by the recoiling of its floating barrels, this weapon lacked the punch of comparable Western cannon, although it proved to be both reliable and robust.

"Red Eagles" pilot Rob "Z-man" Zettel poses beside Ted "Gabby" Drake's MiG-23MS "Flogger-E" "Red 49" at Tonopah. Drake was the 4477th TES's high time "Flogger" instructor pilot with 294 sorties. Although he liked the jet, he was wary of its lethal proclivities. (USAF via Steve Davies)

The type was almost universally reviled by the "Red Eagles" pilots because of its unreliable handling characteristics. On the eve of Operation *Desert Storm*, one former "Red Eagles" pilot summed up the "Flogger" by saying, "When the MiG-23 had first come out, [USAF Intelligence] had told us that this jet was going to be a huge threat to American and Coalition airplanes. They told us it had tremendous capabilities and we should be scared to death of it. From a tactical fighter pilot's point of view, the thing was a piece of junk."

MiG-25 "FOXBAT"

The IrAF received its first "Foxbats" – 12 MiG-25P interceptors and 12 MiG-25R reconnaissance aircraft, as well as six MiG-25PU two-seat trainers – in mid-1980, just prior to initiating the Iran–Iraq War. The early model "Foxbat-A" interceptors were former PVO-Strany equipment, now excess to Soviet requirements. They were poorly equipped, carrying the original (mid-1970s) RP-25 *Smerch-A1* pulse radar and early Bisnovat (later Molniya, then Vympel) R-40 missiles. The Iraqis complained bitterly, demanding more advanced equipment. Indeed, they flatly refused to accept them. The following year a team of Soviet technicians and a shipment of newer RP-25 *Smerch-A2* radars and R-40RD and R-40TD missiles arrived to upgrade the 12 interceptors to MiG-25PDS ("Foxbat-E" export version) standard.

The reason the Soviets were more generous than usual in providing their client states with more modern equipment was that the original *Smerch* radar had been fully compromised by Lt Viktor Belenko's September 1976 defection, flying a nearly new (built in February that year) "Foxbat-A" from Chuguyevka AB (530th IAP of the 20th *Istrebitelniy Aviatsionniy Diviziya,* Fighter Aviation Division, or IAD) near Vladivostok, to Hakodate, Japan.

"Belenko's gift to America" – MiG-25P "Red 31" – after landing at Hakodate airport, in northern Japan, in September 1976. (AP Wirephoto)

Belenko's MiG-25P was equipped with the upgraded *Smerch-A2*, this powerful, I-band, low PRF pulse radar boasting performance similar to the F-4D's AN/APQ-109. Its inverse cassegrain antenna swept +/-30 degrees either side of the aircraft's nose and "looked up" as much as 14 degrees in elevation, but had no "look-down" capability, except at its highest operational altitudes (where the earth's curvature allowed searching beneath the nose by about five degrees). The jet's two engine-driven electrical generators provided its enormous 600KW transmission power, which enabled detection of a Tu-16-size target at 54nm (100km) and the ability to track it from 32nm (60km). The *-A2* upgrade provided improved jamming resistance, increased reliability, and better "low-level clutter tolerance," but according to Belenko, "a MiG-25 cannot distinguish targets below 500m [1,640ft] because of ground clutter." Targets were presented on the K-10T radar scope, and could be acquired ("locked onto") by the pilot, or by GCI via the *Vozdookh-1* command system.

With the system totally compromised by Belenko's "gift to America," making PVO-Strany's primary interceptor vulnerable to exploitation by the USAF, the Soviet air defense service scrambled to replace the *Smerch-A2* with a different sensor suite, choosing to upgrade to the more powerful Sapfir-25 (N005, later redesignated the

Buried deep within the MiG-25P's cockpit is the RP-25 *Smerch-A* ("Tornado A") K-10T radar scope – the black circular object just beyond the top of the stick grip. Due to its positioning, the pilot had to go "heads down" in order to see the information presented and manipulate the radar and weapons controls. (Author's Collection)

RP-25M) and acquiring a limited front-aspect depressed angle capability in doing so. For the improved MiG-25PD, ranges increased to 59nm (110km) for detection and 40nm (74km) for tracking targets level-to-look-up, and provided a 15.4/12.7nm (28.5/23.5km) range in the look-down mode. The new RP-25M was paired with the AVM-25 analog computer and TP-26Sh-1 IRSTS mounted beneath the nose.

The *Smerch-A* radar (NATO name "Foxfire") – a powerful transmitter that Belenko said could "kill [fry] a rabbit at 1,000m". (Foxbat Files)

The MiG-25PD completed its test program and entered production in 1978, with the MiG-25PDS (*Perekhvatchik Dorabotannyy v Stroyou* – "field-modified interceptor") upgrades being installed from early 1979 as MiG-25Ps returned to the Gorky factory for overhaul. Production of/modification to the MiG-25PD/PDS ended in 1982.

The upgrade of their own MiG-25s allowed the Soviets to share the "Foxbat's" previous radar system with its client states, including Iraq. The export version of the MiG-25PD reverted to the *Smerch-A2* radar, with all of its capabilities and limitations, improved with new avionics and an anti-jamming "azimuth only" mode. It could also now carry and employ the Molniya R-60M "dogfight missile." For IFF, the "Foxbat-E" used the SRO-2M transponder and had a SPO-10 Sirena-3 RWR.

The "Foxbat-E" *Eksportnyy* model's primary weapon was the huge Bisnovat R-40, which was produced in both the SAR-homing (R-40RD) and IR-guided (R-40TD) versions. The "Foxbat" carried one of each beneath each wing, with the RP-25 radar slaving the seeker heads of both missiles on that side to the same target. When the R-40RD's seeker "saw" the target (actually the RP-25's reflected radar energy) and the closing velocity, altitude delta (differential – in other words, how high the R-40 had to climb to reach the target), and launch aircraft G-loading were all within prescribed limits, and the range to the target was within the dynamic (flight) range of the missile, the "Ready to Launch" (in-range) cue was illuminated in the cockpit. If fired in "salvo," the R-40TD would launch first so that its IR seeker head would not transfer lock to the rocket plume of the other missile.

The "Foxbat" carried its Bisnovat R-40T heat-seeking missile inboard beneath the wing and the R-40R radar-guided missile outboard, launching the inboard missile first if a "salvo" of weapons was fired. With experiences from the war with Iran teaching the IrAF that the combination of high speed, surprise attack, and a punch from long range offered the best chances of success in air combat, Iraqi MiG-25s were usually armed with four medium-range air-to-air missiles. Coded AA-6 "Acrid" by the ASCC, the R-40RD (semi-active radar homing) and the R-40RT (infra-red homing) medium-range air-to-air missiles proved quite reliable and powerful weapons, capable of knocking out even the most survivable of targets. Depending on aspect of engagement, they were usually fired from ranges between 20 and 30 kilometers. (Foxbat Files)

Until the advent of the US Navy's AIM-54 Phoenix, the 1,016lb (461kg) R-40 was the largest air-to-air missile ever produced. Engineered specifically for high-altitude engagements in thin air, it mounted a large 154lb (70kg) blast-fragmentation warhead. Its rocket motor accelerated the missile to Mach 2 over that of the launch aircraft, and in a direct head-on shot with more than Mach 5 closing velocity, the missile could be fired at a range of 27nm (50km). Capable of sustaining only 2.5Gs, as the angle off the target's nose increased the maximum employment range diminished exponentially, resulting in the missile having no capability aft of the beam (3–9 o'clock line) unless the MiG-25 had a high overtake velocity from astern against a high-altitude/slow-speed target such as the U-2.

The weapon was cleared for employment down to 1,640ft (500m) above ground level (AGL), but the much thicker air drastically reduced the range of the large, heavy missile. Although rated for employment against targets as high as 98,425ft (30,000m), in actuality, according to Belenko, it was "useless [against targets] above 88,580ft (27,000m)" because even the huge fins on the R-40 could not sustain controlled flight in the ultra-thin (0.4psi versus 14.7psi at sea level) atmosphere.

F-15C EAGLE

In 1980–82, while *Heyl Ha'Avir* (Israeli Air Force, IAF) F-15As were shooting down Syrian-flown Soviet-export MiG-21s, MiG-23s, and MiG-25s by the dozens over Lebanon, the USAF deployed its improved F-15Cs to the 36th TFW at Bitburg and the 32nd TFS at Soesterberg. Colloquially known as "Guarding the Ramparts of Freedom," these four NATO-committed USAF in Europe (USAFE) fighter squadrons trained hard to battle and beat the Warsaw Pact's newly arrived MiG-23MF/ML "Flogger-Bs" and "-Gs" that were now equipping a growing number of unit within the Soviet 16th Air Army in East Germany.

The latter included 6th Guards IAD at Merseburg, 16th Guards IAD at Damgarten and 126th IAD at Zerbst, backed up by the 4th Air Army's 239th "Baranovichskaya Red Banner" IAD at Kolobzreg (near Gdansk), in Poland, and 114th "Tallinskiy Red Banner" IAP, part of the 131st "Novgorodskaya Red Banner" Mixed Aviation Division at Milovice, in Czechoslovakia. During this period a Soviet IAD was composed of three 45-aircraft regiments. With these units

The F-15C simulator cockpit. The APG-63 radar scope is to the upper left, just to that side of the stack of HUD, IFF, and UHF radio controls, with the ALR-56C RWR mounted to the upper right. (Steve Davies)

reinforced by "Flogger-Bs" supplied to Czechoslovakia, East Germany, Hungary, Poland, Bulgaria, and Romania, the Americans were outnumbered five-to-one, so the USAFE units' air combat training (ACT) was intense, attempting to maximize the advantages inherent in their new F-15Cs.

According to USAF Technical Order 1F-15A-1-1, the APG-63 was a "high frequency, pulse Doppler attack radar designed primarily for A/A combat". Note the flat, planar array antenna and its T-shaped A/A interrogator transmitters. (USAF)

The first of these was the upgraded Hughes AN/APG-63 radar. This powerful high-frequency (X-band) PD radar could detect fighter-size targets at 80 miles in the look up environment and approximately half that looking below the Eagle's altitude, and was able to track a fighter at about three-quarters those values. The radar sweep and vertical volume was adjustable, but normally a setting of 60 degrees either side of the nose and a ten-degree vertical scan volume was used. At 20 miles the radar search pattern covered 20,000ft of altitude, and a pair of Eagles working in concert could see any aircraft from the earth's surface up to the contrail level at that range.

In the C-model, the APG-63's data processor (its internal computer) was increased to 96K memory, allowing the radar to "remember" the location and vector of one target while the pilot locked up another and could transfer the lock back and forth between the two targets. It was also provided with a programmable signal processor (PSP), enabling the upgrading of the radar's search and tracking logic by merely changing a computer tape. Other enhancements included Doppler beam sharpening, a high-resolution Raid Assessment Mode (RAM), speed-selectable ground moving target indicator (GMTI) and improved electronic counter-countermeasures (ECCM) features.

The Eagle's ECM suite – known as the Tactical Electronic Warfare System (TEWS) – was one of the primary features that allowed the F-15C to enter contested airspace with some measure of protection from SAMs and radar-aimed anti-aircraft artillery (AAA). Mounted in the large "bay" behind the pilot's ACES II ejection seat, the main part of the system was the Northrop AN/ALQ-135 internal countermeasures set (ICS), which provided deception and noise jamming in the H, I, and J bands against a range of AAA and SAM radars and some AI radars, including the "Foxbat's" "Foxfire" radar. Electronically activated by the Loral AN/ALR-56C RWR, the system responded automatically to any adversary lock-on of the aircraft, jamming the enemy emitter while the system's cockpit display alerted the pilot to the threat, allowing him to take evasive action while scanning visually for any incoming missiles. The F-15C pilot also had the new Tracor AN/ALE-40/45 chaff and flare dispensers that could be programmed to activate automatically or could be expended manually by hitting a switch on the outside of the throttles.

The heart of the F-15's weapons system was the IBM CP-1075/AYK central computer, which provided all of the weapons engagement zone (WEZ) depictions to the vertical situation display (VSD, i.e. the radar scope) and HUD and dynamically calculated the maximum, optimum, and minimum firing ranges. With the C-model it, too, was upgraded, increasing its processing speed, enlarging its memory to 34K, and making it reprogrammable, thus permitting changes in the weapons envelopes database, anticipating the arrival of the improved AIM-7M and AIM-9M missiles.

The Raytheon AIM-7F/M was an improved version of the F-4's AIM-7E that had been used over North Vietnam, but with such a dismal effectiveness (9.15 percent) that it was derided as "the great white hope." Twenty years later, the F-15C was still lugging around upgraded versions of the missile while awaiting the AIM-120 Advanced Medium Range Air-to-Air Missile (AMRAAM). The Sparrow's aerodynamic range was very similar to the MiG-23's R-23/R-24 "Apex," depending on the intercept geometry and closure rates during the time of flight of the missile. Although the upgrades had increased its theoretical "probability of kill" (Pk) to 36–45 percent, the accepted firing doctrine was to unleash two missiles about two seconds apart, raising the mathematical probabilities of success up to 54–68 percent, lightening the Eagle (increasing the thrust-to-weight ratio by reducing the latter by 1,020lbs) and giving the MiG pilot something to think about (avoiding).

Similarly, the Raytheon AIM-9L/M was an improved version of the Sidewinder used over North Vietnam. It, too, initially had a disappointing (17.9 percent) effectiveness in that conflict, but the improvements during the next 12 years resulted in an all-aspect heat-seeking missile, eliminating the need to get behind a target to shoot it. The AIM-9L mounted an argon-cooled, high-discrimination Indium Antimonide (InSb) seeker head that could "see" the heat of a jet engine through the

The F-15C carried AIM-9M Sidewinders under the wings and AIM-7M Sparrows on the fuselage stations. (USAF)

F-15C EAGLE ARMAMENT

During Operation *Desert Storm*, USAF F-15Cs carried four AIM-7M Sparrow radar-guided missiles on the fuselage stations and four AIM-9M Sidewinder heat-seeking missiles on rails beneath the wings. Additionally, the fighter mounted a General Electric M61A1 Vulcan 20mm rotary cannon in the right wing root, fed from a large drum in the center of the fuselage. The drum carried 940 rounds of high-explosive incendiary (HEI) ammunition, which was fired at a rate of 6,000 rounds per minute.

aircraft skin even against a warm (ground, sunlit cloud tops, etc.) background. Using a button on the stick, the pilot could "uncage" the missile seeker head, confirm a self-track in the HUD and launch the weapon without taking his radar (which was needed to support AIM-7s in flight) off another target, thus achieving two "kills" during one pass. The missile's range varied with engagement dynamics, but more than adequately filled the void inside the sophisticated AIM-7's minimum range – and its Pk was 75–90 percent, making it a one-shot weapon. The AIM-9M was a "Lima" with flare rejection capability.

Carrying a full suite of four Sparrow SAR-homing missiles and four Sidewinder all-aspect IR-seeking missiles, the Eagle potentially could destroy two adversary aircraft before the two sides "merged" (a GCI term for when opposing fighters met and became one radar plot). With its high thrust-to-weight ratio, the F-15 could be wracked around in a 9G turn – with an instantaneous turn rate of 17.5 degrees/second at 375 knots – or at less G sustain a turn rate of 15 degrees/second continuously at 425 knots. Both of these out-performed the MiG-23 and MiG-25, and provided the potential for the Eagle to maneuver to the inside of the enemy's "turning circle" while bringing the nose – and with it the AIM-9L/M and M61A1 20mm "Gatling gun" – to bear on the target. With a firing rate of 6,000 rounds per minute, and 940 rounds on board, the Eagle's Vulcan cannon could shred a target aircraft in mere seconds.

What made it possible to employ the Eagle in the dynamic, hard-turning, high-G dogfighting environment was the hands-on-throttle-and-stick (HOTAS) interface between the pilot and the jet, and a HUD that presented complete aircraft performance and targeting/firing data to the pilot. The throttles carried the weapons selector switch, where the pilot could command medium- (MRM/AIM-7) or short-ranged (SRM/AIM-9) missiles – each with its own specific radar search pattern optimized for the WEZ of that missile – or the 20mm cannon (GUN), as well as the radar "steering button," the speedbrake, microphone, AAI (air-to-air interrogator), AIM-9 boresight/gunsight reticle stiffen and chaff/flare dispenser buttons.

At longer ranges, in MRM and SRM search, the radar steering button (technically the target designator control or TDC) was used to change the range and sweep of the radar as well as manually acquire (lock on) the target. Once the target was sighted, or during a hard-turning high-G dogfight, radar lock-ons and subsequent weapons employment were facilitated by pulling the Eagle's nose towards the target and using a choice of four automatic-acquisition (AutoAcq) modes – selected by a multi-function switch on the stick and each with a volume display presented on the HUD – to lock onto the target. The pilot had only to place the target within the displayed (usually circular) volume and the radar would lock on automatically; then the pilot would select the proper weapon – MRM/SRM/GUN – for the engagement situation (range and angles) and begin firing when in that weapons' WEZ.

Flying a very maneuverable, heavily armed fighter equipped with a powerful radar and a high-speed computer with which the pilot interacted almost seamlessly through HOTAS and HUD made the F-15C an air superiority fighter that would soon rule the skies over Iraq.

F-15C Eagle, MiG-23, and MiG-25 Comparison Specifications			
	MiG-23ML	**F-15C Eagle**	**MiG-25PDS**
Powerplant	One 28,665lbs thrust Khachaturov R35F-300 turbojet	Two 23,450lbs thrust Pratt & Whitney F100-PW-220 turbofans	Two 24,691lbs thrust Tumansky R15B-300 turbojets
Dimensions			
Wingspan	16-degree sweep – 45ft 9in 72-degree sweep – 25ft 6in	42ft 10in	46ft
Length	54ft 9in	63ft 9in	64ft 9.5in
Height	14ft 9in	18ft 8in	21ft 4in
Wing Area	45-degree sweep – 384.32 sq. ft	608 sq. ft	660.67sq. ft
Weights			
Empty	22,560lbs	28,600lbs	44,080lbs
Loaded	39,250lbs	57,000lbs	76,984lbs
Thrust-to-Weight*	.956:1	1.16:1	.75:1
Wing Loading*	75.2 lb/sq. ft	66.4 lb/sq. ft	99.4 lb/sq. ft
Performance			
Maximum Speed	756 knots at sea level 1,350 knots at 41,000ft	669 knots at sea level 1,433 knots at 36,000ft	648 knots at sea level 1,620 knots at 42,650ft
Maximum Mach	2.35 above 36,000ft	2.5	2.83
Combat Radius	530 miles	1,060 miles with CFTs	186 miles
Initial Climb Rate	42,312ft/min	approximately 40,000 ft/min	40,950 ft/min
Service Ceiling	61,030ft	60,000ft	67,913ft
Armament	Two R-24 SAR missiles Four R-60M IR missiles One GSh-23L 23mm cannon with 200 rounds	Four AIM-7M SAR and Four AIM-9M IR missiles One GE M61A1 Vulcan 20mm with 940 rounds	Two R-40RD SAR missiles Two R-40TD IR missiles No internal gun
Radar/Fire Control System (ranges are for a fighter-size target)	Sapfir-23D-III (N003E) Detection Range: 24 nm Track Range: 18 nm Limited depressed angle capability	Hughes APG-63 Detection Range: 80 nm Track Range: 60 nm Look-down/Shoot-down capability	*Smerch-A2* Detection Range: 54 nm Track Range: 32 nm No look-down capability

Note – Thrust-to-Weight and Wing Loading calculations use "combat weight," which is after external tanks are jettisoned, 60 percent internal fuel remaining, and with full ordnance load. Thrust is calculated at sea level.

THE STRATEGIC SITUATION

While USAFE's four squadrons of F-15s faced four Soviet V-VS fighter divisions across the "Iron Curtain" that bisected Germany, at the northern end of the Persian Gulf, Iraqi dictator Saddam Hussein decided to attack Iran. The IrAF launched its opening air strike on September 22, 1980, MiG-23BNs and other fighter-bombers attempting to crater runways at eight major Islamic Republic of Iran Air Force (IRIAF) bases and thus prevent any IRIAF response for 48 hours. Largely unaffected, the Iranians struck back early that afternoon, and returned the next morning with a massive 140-aircraft strike. When the Iraqi army launched its offensive into Iran's oil-rich Khuzestan Province, the IRIAF counterattacked with all available aircraft, starting a battle of attrition that proved very costly for both sides.

The IrAF acquired 55 MiG-23MLs from 1984, the aircraft entering service with three squadrons and seeing employment exclusively as interceptors during the war with Iran. This example (serial number 23255) was photographed while undergoing an overhaul in the USSR in 1990. (Ali Tobchi via Tom Cooper)

While initially taking a "wait and see" attitude and withholding further shipments of arms and aircraft to Iraq, the Soviets changed their stance in 1982 and began re-supplying Baghdad again. Reinforcements included 16 MiG-23MFs the next year, with deliveries of the more effective MiG-23ML beginning the year after that. For the rest of the war Iraqi "Floggers" flew a large number of intercept missions over the frontlines, claiming to have shot down four IRIAF Northrop F-5Es and some helicopters, but losses were heavy.

The MiG-25R was the first "Foxbat" variant to become operational with the IrAF (No. 87 Sqn was established with four examples on August 18, 1981), and the aircraft provided excellent service in the Iraq–Iran War – only two were lost in combat. During July 1990, No. 87 Sqn's "Foxbat-Bs" flew four uncontested photo-reconnaissance missions over Kuwait, taking some 800 images of key facilities. (USAF)

While the MiG-25s were received in 1980, little was done to make them operational until the Soviets resumed their support two years later. Once its interceptors were upgraded to MiG-25PDS standard, No. 97 Sqn was activated on the type at Tammuz AB – the center of IrAF air defense operations – in early 1983. Known to US and British military forces as Al Taqaddum AB, Tammuz AB incorporated the former RAF Habbaniyah airfield into its complex. Two years later, following deliveries of ten additional MiG-25PDs and six MiG-25PUs, No. 96 Sqn was established.

The IrAF "Foxbats" began flying operational missions over Iran, sometimes imitating MiG-25RB reconnaissance missions to lure IRIAF F-14As and F-4Es into attempting to intercept them. Iraqi "Foxbat" pilots claimed 19 "kills" by the end of the war, five of which have been verified – an F-4E over Iran, an RF-4E over Iraq, an F-5E, a Fokker F27 airliner carrying Iranian parliamentarians, and a Grumman Gulfstream III carrying an Algerian peace envoy. In return, two MiG-25PDSs were lost in combat, one in July 1986 to an F-5E and the second in March 1988 to an F-4E-launched AIM-7E.

That same year the world's major powers finally lost patience with both sides due to the loss of oil imports and the extensive damage to Western tankers passing through the Persian Gulf. UN Security Council Resolution 598 of August 20, 1988 called for a ceasefire that finally ended hostilities the next month.

Meanwhile, bankrupted by the Cold War arms race, the Soviet Union collapsed and the Warsaw Pact crumbled, resulting in the reunification of Germany on October 3, 1990. Almost overnight, the Communist threat from the East had evaporated, suddenly making a host of military forces – including the four F-15 Eagle squadrons in USAFE – excess to the NATO's needs and now available to counter other threats to Western security.

In an extraordinary example of bad timing, Saddam Hussein picked just this moment in history to attack Kuwait. Demanding that Kuwait pardon at least part of Iraq's $80billion war debt and upset that the Kuwaitis were pumping crude oil from beneath Iraqi territory, Saddam resorted to military force when negotiations failed,

Five fully armed F-15Cs of the 58th TFS "Gorillas" taxi out for takeoff at Eglin AFB in August 1990 at the start of the unit's combat deployment to Saudi Arabia. Within a week of Iraq's conquest of Kuwait, CENTAF had 45 Eagles, 19 F-15E Strike Eagles, and 24 F-16C Fighting Falcons "in theater", ready to respond to further aggression by Saddam Hussein. (USAF)

invading the small emirate on August 2, 1990. Defended by four squadrons of Dassault Mirage F1CKs and McDonnell Douglas A-4KU Skyhawks and a small army, the nation was overrun – by 30,000 troops and 350 tanks – in less than 48 hours. US President George Bush Snr, in concert and consultation with the government of Saudi Arabia, who feared they might be next on Saddam's list of intended victims, ordered the US Central Command (CENTCOM) and its air component, CENTAF, to respond quickly and with impressive, highly visible force.

Five days later the 1st TFW deployed two of its three squadrons to Dhahran AB, in Saudi Arabia. The 71st TFS led the way with 24 F-15Cs and three F-15Ds, all loaded with "wall-to-wall" missiles and "three bags of gas," and, after 15.5 hours of flying time and seven aerial refuelings, arrived on August 7. They were followed the very next day by 25 more fully armed F-15C/Ds from the 27th TFS. Later that same month the 58th TFS "Gorillas" – a heavily augmented "super squadron" equipped with the newest, most advanced version of the F-15C – deployed to King Faisal AB at Tabuk, in the northwest corner of Saudi Arabia.

Anticipating an intense, dynamic, and round-the-clock preparatory aerial campaign, these CENTAF units were joined by USAFE's 53rd TFS "Tigers" (36th TFW) – another "super squadron" – which deployed to Prince Sultan AB ("PSAB," also known as Al Kharj) on December 20, 1990. Once Turkey consented to allowing Coalition aircraft to fly from its bases, Bitburg's 525th TFS "Bulldogs" provided the basis for an additional air superiority squadron organized to cover the "northern front," flying from Incirlik AB. With 14 Bitburg F-15Cs and a contingent of six jets and 12 pilots from the Holland-based 32nd TFS "Wolfhounds," the 32 "Eagle Drivers" at "the 'Lik'" became known as "the War Dogs." Iraq and its air force were now surrounded by Eagles.

To meet them, by January 1991, the MiG-29 "Fulcrum" had replaced the older MiGs as the nation's primary air defense interceptor, 29 of which were assigned to Nos. 6 and 39 Sqns based at Tammuz and Qadessiya ABs, respectively, augmented by the IrAF's 19 MiG-25PD/PDS (Nos. 96 and 97 Sqns), also split between these two airfields. The 40 MiG-23MLs (Nos. 63, 73, and 93 Sqns) were considered second-line interceptors, based at al-Bakr AB, north of Baghdad, with detachments deployed to bases around the nation's periphery. The Air Defense force was backed up by 63 modern, multi-role Mirage F1EQs (Nos. 79, 81, 89 and 91 Sqns) and approximately 60 obsolete MiG-21s in four operational squadrons (Nos. 9, 14, 37, and 47 Sqns).

Numerically, the force ratios – 118 USAF F-15Cs versus 151 modern MiGs and Mirages – were about even, so the decisive factors would be the opponents' sortie generation capabilities, the relative merits of their equipment, and the training, preparation, and aggressiveness of the men that flew them.

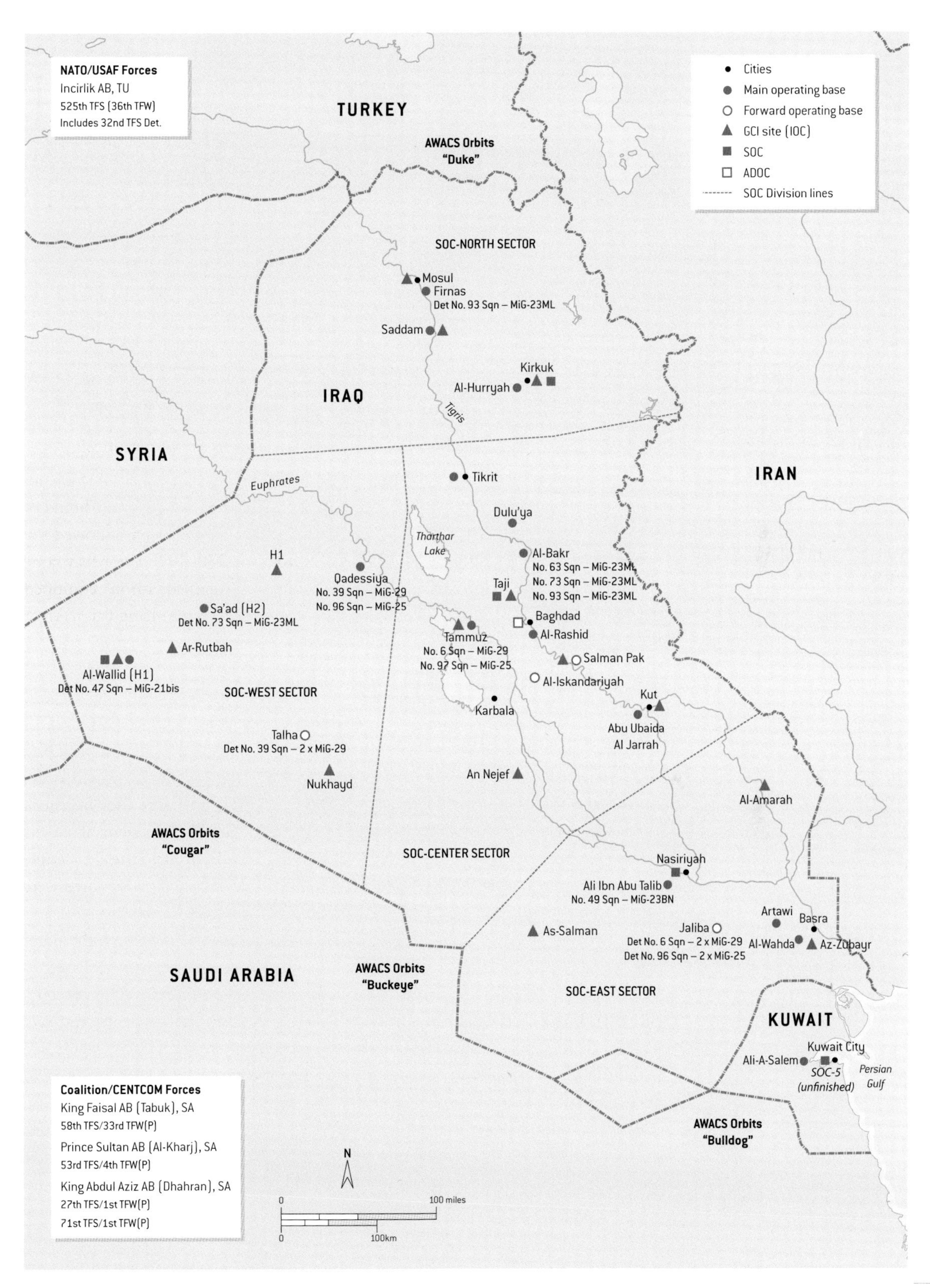

NATO/USAF Forces
Incirlik AB, TU
525th TFS (36th TFW)
Includes 32nd TFS Det.
TURKEY
AWACS Orbits "Duke"
Cities
Main operating base
Forward operating base
GCI site (IOC)
SOC
ADOC
SOC Division lines
SOC-NORTH SECTOR
Mosul
Firnas
Det No. 93 Sqn – MiG-23ML
Saddam
Kirkuk
Al-Hurryah
IRAQ
Tigris
SYRIA
Tikrit
IRAN
Euphrates
Dulu'ya
Tharthar Lake
H1
Qadessiya
No. 39 Sqn – MiG-29
No. 96 Sqn – MiG-25
Al-Bakr
No. 63 Sqn – MiG-23ML
No. 73 Sqn – MiG-23ML
No. 93 Sqn – MiG-23ML
Taji
Sa'ad (H2)
Det No. 73 Sqn – MiG-23ML
Baghdad
Al-Rashid
Tammuz
No. 6 Sqn – MiG-29
No. 97 Sqn – MiG-25
Ar-Rutbah
Al-Wallid (H1)
Det No. 47 Sqn – MiG-21bis
Salman Pak
Al-Iskandariyah
SOC-WEST SECTOR
Kut
Karbala
Abu Ubaida Al Jarrah
Talha
Det No. 39 Sqn – 2 x MiG-29
Nukhayd
An Nejef
Al-Amarah
AWACS Orbits "Cougar"
SOC-CENTER SECTOR
Nasiriyah
Ali Ibn Abu Talib
No. 49 Sqn – MiG-23BN
Artawi
Basra
As-Salman
Jaliba
Det No. 6 Sqn – 2 x MiG-29
Det No. 96 Sqn – 2 x MiG-25
Al-Wahda
Az-Zubayr
SAUDI ARABIA
AWACS Orbits "Buckeye"
SOC-EAST SECTOR
KUWAIT
Kuwait City
Ali-A-Salem
SOC-5 (unfinished)
Persian Gulf
Coalition/CENTCOM Forces
King Faisal AB (Tabuk), SA
58th TFS/33rd TFW(P)
Prince Sultan AB (Al-Kharj), SA
53rd TFS/4th TFW(P)
King Abdul Aziz AB (Dhahran), SA
27th TFS/1st TFW(P)
71st TFS/1st TFW(P)
AWACS Orbits "Bulldog"
N
0
100 miles
0
100km

THE COMBATANTS

IRAF FIGHTER PILOT TRAINING

As a British-mandated territory during the "golden age of aviation" – from 1920 to 1931 – the IrAF inherited its initial organizational structure, training programs, uniforms, and traditions from the Royal Air Force (RAF). It maintained a presence at RAF Habbaniyah, in the center of the country, and RAF Shaibah (renamed al-Wahda AB after the British left, in 1955), 24 miles south of Basra. However, by 1936 the Royal Iraqi Air Force had begun making its own way, and by 1958, when a military coup assassinated young King Feisal and overthrew the Hashemite monarchy, the air arm began using Soviet bloc equipment in its combat forces and training programs.

Like most air forces, pilot training was a three-phase process – ab initio training in light propeller-powered trainers, basic jet flying training, and advanced training in higher performance jet aircraft. By the mid-1970s the IrAF was using Czechoslovakian aircraft – Zlin Z-526 tandem seat light trainers, Aero Vodochody L-29 Delfíns ("Dolphin"), and the more advanced Aero L-39 Albatros high-performance jet trainers.

IrAF pilot training began at the Flight Academy, a part of the Iraqi Military College, which was moved to the expansive new Tikrit AB, near Bayji, 135 miles north of Baghdad, in 1974. All Iraqi armed forces officers were graduates of the Military College, and the top volunteers meeting the IrAF's physical and aptitude pilot requirements were inducted into the pilot training program. Political, religious, and ethnic backgrounds also mattered. The IrAF was dominated by the Sunnis, who flew the most advanced and

Between 1968 and 1974 the IrAF purchased 78 Aero L-29 Delfin jet trainers, the type being heavily utilized for basic jet training at the Air Force Academy in Tikrit. (Tom Cooper Collection)

sophisticated fighter and bomber aircraft, while the very few Shi'a admitted were generally channelled into the MiG-23BN air-to-ground units. The Kurds were unlikely to serve in combat units, most of them becoming transport pilots.

The flight training program at Tikrit lasted three years, with new pilots graduating with approximately 400 hours of flying time, after which they trained for another year in their assigned aircraft type, gaining a further 100 hours of experience during their conversion. Interceptor pilots were initially assigned to the MiG-21, a nearly viceless and exciting high-performance jet to fly – perfect for young, inexperienced aviators learning their trade – and were trained on the Shenyang F-7B and FT-7 (Chinese copies of the obsolete MiG-21F-13/-21U "Fishbed-C" and "Mongol-A") with No. 7 Sqn/OCU. Once new pilots had gained experience in their operational unit, they were considered for assignment to higher-performance interceptors, the MiG-23 and MiG-25.

When the IrAF negotiated to acquire its first "Floggers," a cadre of MiG-21 pilots (along with ground technicians) were selected and sent to the Lugovaya training center near Frunze (Buishkek), in the USSR. The Russians did not acknowledge the Iraqis' considerable flying experience – all had at least 1,500 hours in fast jets – and treated them like neophyte cadets. Historically heavily invested in the theoretical and academic side of flight training, the V-VS syllabus spent four months teaching various courses, from the most basic to the more technical, with only two months of flying training, without any tactical lectures or live-firing exercises.

The first group of IrAF pilots trained on the MiG-25 consisted of 14 pilots who went to the USSR for conversion training on March 19, 1980. All of these completed conversion training on the two-seat MiG-25PU and five continued in a specialized reconnaissance course on the MiG-25RB. Weapons and tactics training on the MiG-25PD/PDS was conducted at Tammuz, with the first unit – No. 97 Sqn – being established there in 1983. A second unit – No. 96 Sqn – was also initially established at Tammuz in 1985 and became operational the following year, transferring to Qadissiya in 1987.

Student pilot 2Lt Jay T. Denney poses in front of a trusty Northrop T-38A Talon at Reese AFB in 1984. (Col Jay Denney via Author)

USAF FIGHTER PILOT TRAINING

Selected from recent college graduates of American universities, the USAF Academy (USAFA), and those attending Officer Candidate School (OCS), pilot candidates underwent an intense, regimented, and highly competitive year-long training program known as Undergraduate Pilot Training (UPT). Prior to admission, the candidates were screened at their colleges/USAFA/OCS by flying modified Cessna 172s in USAF markings (called T-41s) or similar civilian light aircraft. Those that possessed the aptitude were admitted into UPT, where the USAF's demanding flying training truly began.

Typical of this process was 2Lt Jay T. Denney, a 1983 graduate of Auburn University who easily passed the school's screening program in the Piper PA-28-140 Cherokee. Attending UPT at Reese AFB, Lubbock, Texas, Denney completed 81 hours in the Cessna T-37B "Tweet" and 101 hours in the Northrop T-38A Talon. After another 38 hours of basic tactical training in the AT-38B "Attack Talon," Denney proceeded to Luke AFB, Phoenix, Arizona, for F-15 training with the 555th TFTS, before being assigned to the 58th TFS at Eglin AFB. The day after his Mission Ready check ride, he flew his first "Constant Peg" sortie, training against a 4477th TES MiG-21.

As Denney explained, "'Constant Peg' was a great program to demonstrate the limitations of the MiGs. However, the most important aspect of our training was flying Dissimilar Air Combat Training (DACT), fighting those who do not fight the same way we do – the Navy, Marines, and foreign air forces. The more you saw, the more tools you had. Just like boxers preparing for various fighters. Before *Desert Storm* we were able to deploy to France and fight against the Mirage F1C. We also trained against East German MiG-29s through a special liaison."

Getting prepared for *Desert Storm*, operational training continued even more intensely. Denney, who was by this time one of the 36th TFW's weapons officers, added, "We [53rd TFS] designated paired four ships and built a training plan that started in October, with emphasis on large force missions flown in Germany's Northern TRAs [Temporary Reserved Airspace]. I was able to convince the wing leadership that we needed to conduct night training 'lights out,' and we were able to do so on some occasions. This proved to be very effective in helping us to develop our tactics."

IRAF MiG-23 AND MiG-25 TACTICS

The MiG-23 and MiG-25 were Soviet interceptors designed to destroy individual USAF supersonic tactical (F-111) and strategic (XB-70) bombers carrying nuclear

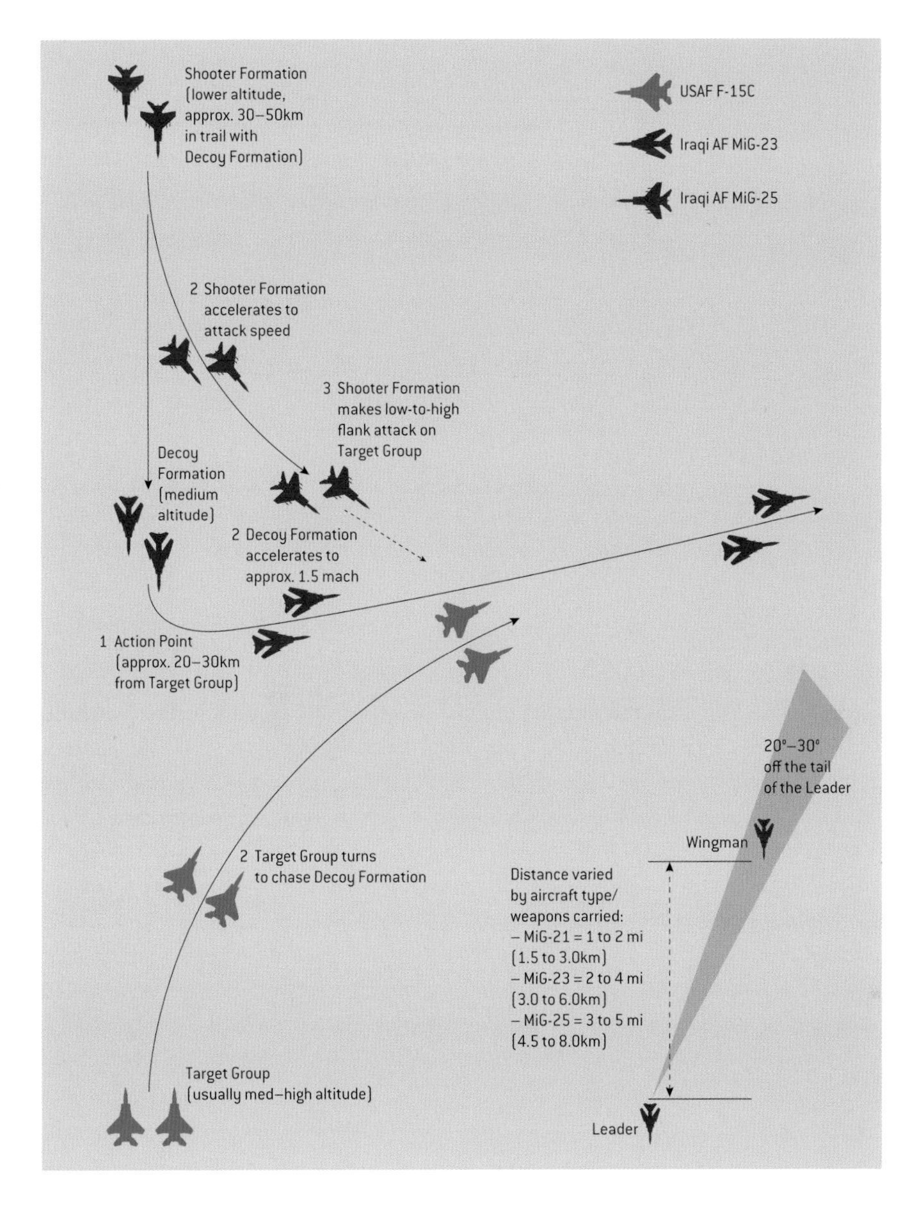

For air-to-air combat, the basic IrAF combat tactic replicated the typical Soviet MiG "Lead Around" or "decoy" maneuver, using two widely separated, independently vectored two-ships in the *e pare patrul* ("paired patrol") formation. GCI vectored the leading (decoy) formation onto the extended flightpath (off the nose of) the "target group" before closing "head on" to an "action point" approximately 20–30km (10.8–16.2nm) in front of the targets. The decoys would then be turned away 90–120 degrees to one side and vectored towards a safe area – usually housing a SAM unit – and accelerate to remain beyond the "target group's" weapons. The shooter formation would be vectored independently by GCI to follow the decoys at approximately 30–50km (16.2–27nm) and, after the decoys turned away, they would be vectored to a firing position on the "target group's" flank and would then be told to turn on their radars, where to look to locate the targets, and to open fire.

Typically, due to poor cockpit visibility in all directions except forward, Soviet MiGs flew a "paired patrol" two-ship formation, with the wingman being well aft of the leader while maintaining position/distance in a dynamic 20–30-degree cone around the leader's tail. The distance was predicated by the range of the air-to-air missiles carried by the various fighter types, so that the wingman would be in the "heart of the envelope" for the ordnance his MiG was carrying, thus enabling him to shoot any attacker "off the tail" of his leader.

weapons. This mission meant that they were almost completely dependent upon GCI controllers to locate and direct them to their targets. Furthermore, these limitations meant that the MiG pilots lacked any BVR awareness of the location of enemy fighters, or of other friendly aircraft – in other words, they lacked "situational awareness" (SA) – without GCI information.

Providing IrAF MiGs with SA, target information, and attack vectors was a fairly sophisticated and geographically comprehensive integrated air defense system (IADS) called KARI. It linked 75 radar units – Soviet-made P-15/-15M2/-18 (NATO "Flat Face," "Squat Eye," and "Spoon Rest") early warning (EW) and P-35M/-37 "Saturn" (NATO "Bar Lock") GCI radars, plus a few French TRS-2100 Tiger S tactical "gap-fillers" – and 648 "visual observatories" with 15 Intercept Operations Centers (IOCs – GCI director units), five (counting the new, incomplete one in occupied Kuwait)

F-15 pilots practiced "getting away from the smoke trail" by immediately turning 45–50 degrees to one side – called an "f-pole maneuver" – that would slow their arrival at the "merge" and "stiff-arm" the opponent's missile. (Gary Klett via Steve Davies)

air battle management Sector Operations Centers (SOCs), and the national Air Defense Operations Center (ADOC) in Baghdad.

Development of KARI (French for "Iraq" spelled backwards) began in the late 1970s when the IrAF first realized the need for a centralized, semi-automated IADS. The Soviets were unable or unwilling to provide the required technologies – especially computer systems – but the French Thomson-CSF (now Thales) company possessed the necessary expertise, technologies, and willingness to share/sell them. Regular and effective low-altitude attacks by IRIAF F-4D/Es during autumn 1980, and the June 1981 Israeli attack on the construction site of nuclear reactors in Tuwaitha, underscored the urgency in completing this system. It was finished six years later.

Consistent with Soviet air defense doctrine, KARI was organized on a hierarchical basis that channeled information up from EW radars, GCI units, SAMs, and ELINT/SIGINT-gathering stations through the SOCs, with orders flowing downwards from the ADOC, but with little information being passed laterally between the SOCs. It was designed to engage raids of 20–40 aircraft penetrating an individual sector – from Israel or Iran for example – not to meet massive air attacks flooding multiple sectors simultaneously.

The SOC/GCI/SAM network in each quadrant was organized into an Air Defense Sector (ADS), two of which covered Iraq's 646-mile-long southern border with Saudi Arabia. In the west, guarding the main "H2/H3 Complex" airfields (al-Wallid, Sa'ad, and three dispersal fields) and Saddam's western surface-to-surface missile (Scud) brigade was the 2nd ADS, which operated SOC-West (at al-Wallid AB/H3) and three IOCs. To the southeast was the 3rd ADS, with its SOC-South at Nasiriyah and three IOCs.

Protecting Baghdad and central Iraq was the 1st ADS – its SOC-Center was in the large military complex at Taji – which had six IOCs arrayed around the capital and controlled "Fulcrums" and "Foxbats" (Nos. 6 and 96 Sqns, respectively) based at

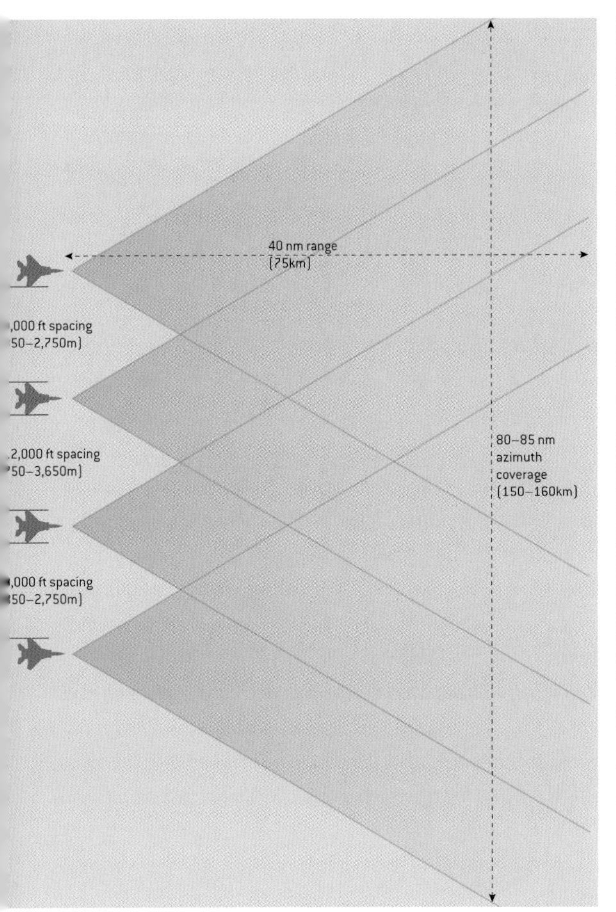

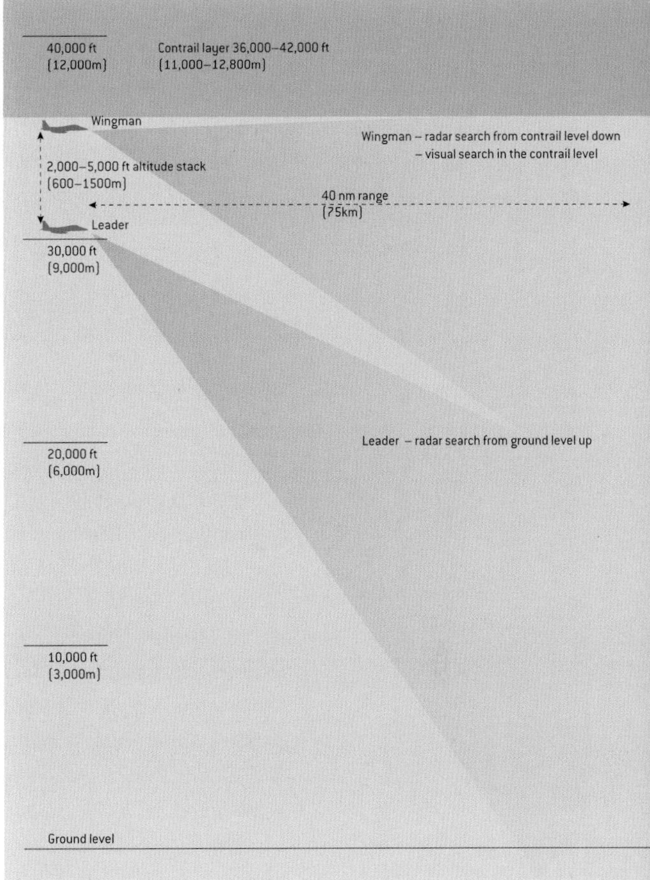

The primary F-15C four-ship fighting formation was the "Wall of Eagles" composed of two pairs, or "elements," in line-abreast formation. The element leaders (#1 and #3) were on the "inside" of the formation and the wingmen (#2 and #4) manned the flanks. Using their radars, all formation members searched the area ahead of them usually in a 120-degree azimuth sweep, which covered an 80nm-wide arc at 40 miles off the nose. With as much as five miles between the wingmen, at 40nm the entire formation searched an 85-mile-wide swath, making it difficult for an adversary to outflank the formation, or escape detection. Nevertheless, the element leaders were responsible for checking the "six o'clock" of their wingmen, and the wingmen in turn split their attention between their radars and scanning around the flanks of the formation to visually detect any adversary that may have slipped through the radar coverage.

Each two-ship element in the "Wall of Eagles" formation searched with their radars from the earth's surface to the base of the contrail level, the two elements ensuring overlapping coverage. Additionally, the wingman visually scanned the contrail layer for telltale signs of aircraft approaching in that altitude band.

Tammuz, with MiG-23MLs (No. 63 Sqn) based at al-Bakr AB (Balad SE). Guarding the northern border was the 4th ADS/SOC-North, which had three IOCs, and was primarily equipped with Mirage F1EQ multi-role fighter-bombers.

Iraqi interception tactics were heavily influenced by experiences from the war with Iran and cooperation with the French. While the majority of Iraqi interceptor pilots were trained only for operations under strict GCI control, the more experienced ones – especially those with combat experience against the Iranians and/or who had attended specialist courses abroad – were much more capable. Most of their combat maneuvers were variations of those published in French and Soviet tactical manuals, adapted according to their own experiences, preferences, and local circumstances. Contrary to usual reports, some IrAF pilots did train in dynamic, "free-style" dogfighting that characterized American and British air combat training, but only as "back up." Aware of the limitations of PD radar when it came to tracking targets "in the beam," they developed corresponding "notch" tactics to "break the lock" of the F-15C's APG-63 radar.

USAF F-15 TACTICS

American F-15Cs flying into hostile airspace also needed a long-range look into that airspace in order to provide SA, target locations, and initial attack vectors. These were provided by the USAF's 552nd Airborne Warning and Control Wing's Boeing E-3B/C Sentry, five of which were stationed at Riyadh. Commonly called the Airborne Warning and Control System (AWACS), the E-3's AN/APY-1 pulse radar had an over-the-horizon "look range" of approximately 350nm (650km) for aircraft flying at medium to high altitudes, while its pulse-Doppler radar could see low-altitude targets out to 215nm (400km). These aircraft were augmented by five Royal Saudi Air Force (RSAF) Sentries from No. 18 Sqn, also based at Riyadh. Together, the AWACS would continuously man three orbits – with a fourth E-3 as airborne reserve – along the Saudi–Iranian border, from where they were able to "see" beyond Baghdad. A fifth AWACS orbiting over Turkey watched the northern half of Iraq, allowing complete surveillance of the country.

Typically, USAF F-15s operated as a four-ship formation (or "flight") and would ingress line abreast in what was known as "a wall of Eagles." Using a commonly known geographical reference point, AWACS would present a "picture," calling the location of airborne targets with direction and distance from the "bullseye," adding altitude and any other specific information, such as aircraft type, if known. The Eagles would be "paired" against any IrAF fighter threatening them or the strike packages that commonly followed the ingressing F-15s. Once the Eagles acquired radar locks on the adversary target(s), the four-ship flight leader would establish the intercept direction, especially to cut off the Iraqis from getting to the strikers, assign targeting responsibilities, and ensure the radar contacts were identified as "bandits." Once in range, each two-ship ("element") transitioned to independent tactics, missiles would start flying and, upon arriving at the merge, hard, coordinated maneuvering ensued to achieve shooting parameters (WEZ) against the surviving MiGs.

Once temporary, local air superiority was achieved by defeating the IrAF's "first responders," CAP patterns would be established, oriented to face the air bases from which the next threat was expected to be launched. The flight would split into two elements, alternating their "hot" legs (pointed at the target airfield) in the orbit to ensure one Eagle formation was looking at the threat location at all times. Similarly, the AWACS orbits and tanker tracks south of the border were guarded by two-ship CAPs of Eagles in order to protect these "high value assets" (HVAs) and provide reserves for the F-15s engaged over Iraq.

JAY T. DENNEY

The son of a US Army Aviator who flew O-1 Birddogs, C-7 Caribou, UH-1 helicopters, and AH-1 Cobra gunships in four combat tours during the Vietnam War, Jay T. Denney attended Auburn University, Alabama, where he participated in the USAF ROTC program and graduated in March 1983, with honors. Wanting to be a fighter pilot since he was 12, Denney excelled as well in UPT at Reese AFB, Texas, finishing as a Distinguished Graduate and being rewarded with an F-15 assignment. Following Eagle training at Luke AFB, the 22-year-old 2nd lieutenant reported for duty at Eglin AFB in March 1984. An outstanding fighter pilot in every respect, Denney rose quickly, qualifying as an instructor, evaluator, and mission commander while still a 1st lieutenant and earning a follow-on assignment to the 53rd TFS "Tigers." Within six months of arriving at Bitburg AB, he was selected for the intensely demanding Fighter Weapons Instructor course at Nellis AFB, winning the Outstanding Graduate Award.

Returning to the "Tigers," Denney was the squadron weapons officer until June 1990, when he became one of the wing weapons officers for the 36th TFW. Denney was training for the USAF "William Tell" weapons competition when the event was cancelled due to the Iraqi invasion of Kuwait, the "Tigers" deploying to "PSAB" shortly thereafter.

Following Operation *Desert Storm*, Denney continued his exceptional career, commanding the 60th FS "Crows" and the 33rd Operations Group before finally retiring in 2005 after serving as the 1st FW's vice-commander.

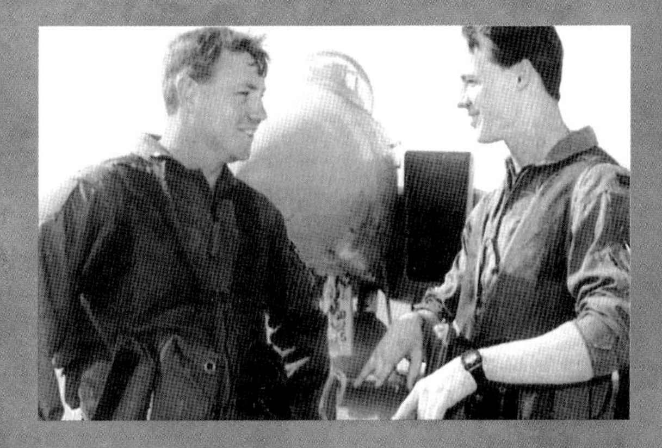

Capts Jay "OP" Denney (right) and wingman Dean "Coma" Powell conduct an impromptu debriefing following their successful engagement against four IrAF fighter-bombers. (Jay Denney via Authors)

MiG-25 PILOTS

Because of severe and clear threats to the personal security of surviving Iraqi fighter pilots, the authors do not feel free to single out any one of them, or provide personal data. From 2003, agents of the Iranian Revolutionary Guards Corps (IRGC) and their Shi'a allies in Iraq began systematically hunting and killing veteran IrAF aviators and officers. A number of them managed to escape to Syria, but several were arrested and jailed there without a trial. Most of them are still languishing in local prisons, usually without contact with their families or absolutely minimal contact with the outside world. They have no lawyers and they do not get to hear from any judge or prosecutor, their guards informing them about the time remaining on their "sentences." Some also escaped to Jordan, only to be kidnapped and "disappeared" – supposedly by Israeli agents. The few that managed to reach Egypt or the West enjoy relative safety, but are still uneasy when contacted by foreigners.

Most of the early Iraqi MiG-25 pilots came from other fighter units – primarily MiG-21s – with a few who had flown MiG-21R reconnaissance jets. During the mid-1980s, several more joined the MiG-25 units after serving with squadrons equipped with MiG-23s. By 1991, nearly all of the approximately 40 pilots qualified to fly MiG-25s were seasoned veterans of the war with Iran – some of those that flew MiG-25RBs had logged up to 200 combat sorties. Most of the "Foxbat" pilots were considered by their peers flying other Iraqi fighters to be well trained and experienced, motivated and competent.

This photograph – of five IrAF Foxbat pilots and MiG-25PDS 2521 (later re-serialled 25221) – attests to the security precautions needed to protect the identities of the surviving Iraqi fighter pilots. (Tom Cooper Collection)

COMBAT

The opening round of Operation *Desert Storm* began at 0300hrs on the night of January 17, 1991 with the first wave – ten F-117s "stealth fighters" of the 37th TFW – penetrating deep into Iraq intent on destroying key elements of the KARI IADS command and control system. In and around Baghdad, seven Nighthawks struck 13 targets with 2,000lb GBU-27 laser-guided bombs (LGBs), hitting the IrAF HQ building, SOC-Center's bunker at Taji, and the Salman Pak IOC, while an eighth attacked SOC-South's bunker at Abu Talib AB. Although hitting their targets, the LGBs failed to penetrate the nuclear-hardened ADOC, and, except for disruptions in electrical power and communications caused by other attacks, it successfully remained "online" throughout the initial blows.

Earlier, at 0238hrs, in the west, "Task Force Normandy" – nine US Army AH-64A Apache attack helicopters led by three USAF MH-53Js of the 20th Special Operations Squadron – began demolishing two of the 2nd ADS's frontline P-15/-18 early warning (EW) radar sites near Ma'anya, 30 miles into Iraqi territory, with AGM-114 Hellfire missiles. Thirteen minutes later, 30 miles northeast of the radar sites, two F-117s blasted the bunkers containing the associated Nukhayb IOC, these three attacks creating a 60-mile-wide hole in the SOC-West's low-altitude radar coverage. The F-117s then flew west to attack the 2nd ADC's SOC at al-Wallid AB, but both bombs missed, allowing the SOC to scramble and control its "first response" interceptors – one MiG-29 (No. 39 Sqn) and two Mirage F1EQs (No. 79 Sqn) launched from Sa'ad AB to establish CAP orbits near ab-Rutbah IOC and southeast of the air base.

Ingressing at 400 ft AGL (above ground level) and 540 knots through this breach flew the first in a series of "packages" – 21 F-15E Strike Eagles of the 4th TFW(P), supported by two EF-111A Raven stand-off jammers from the 390th ECS – targeting 26 fixed Scud missile launchers in the "H2/H3 Complex" area. They were followed an hour later by 13 Panavia Tornados (nine RAF and four RSAF) and 12 F-111Fs from the 48th TFW(P) fanning out to attack Iraqi airfields.

The first mission following the famous F-117 strikes on KARI facilities throughout Iraq was flown by 21 F-15E Strike Eagles. Here, two jets from the 336th TFS "Rocketeers" have their dozen 500lb Mk 82s armed immediately prior to their dusk takeoff from PSAB. (Jerry Oney via Steve Davies)

Just south of the Saudi border, three squadrons of F-15Cs waited for the F-15Es to begin their exits before sweeping into Iraqi airspace to attack any enemy interceptors pursuing the egressing fighter-bombers. From west to east, the 58th TFS "Gorillas" faced four airfields west of Baghdad (al-Wallid, Sa'ad, Talha, and Qadessiya) with eight Eagles, the 53rd TFS "Tigers" covered the central sector (Tammuz) with another four and the 71st TFS swept north into eastern Iraq, including Baghdad, with eight more.

Seeing the MiG-29s and Mirages airborne in the target area, AWACS (callsign "Cougar") sent the western F-15Cs across the border 15 minutes earlier than planned. Leading the way was Capt Rick "Kluso" Tollini, 58th TFS weapons officer, with his four-ship of F-15Cs. Looking northwest, Tollini's formation ("Penzoil 61") detected "several individual IrAF CAPs located north and west of the egressing train of F-15Es and in the vicinity of H2/H3. Sample locks with our radars resulted in the Iraqi fighters turning away, with only one approaching close enough for me to direct 'Cherry' ["Penzoil 62"/Capt Larry Pitts] to investigate by leaning in its direction until it too eventually broke off towards the Syrian border.

"As tempting as it was to pursue the wandering IrAF fighters, our job that night was to continue north and sweep the area west of Baghdad. Our patience would shortly be rewarded with a 'pop-up' contact [another MiG-29] climbing fast towards us from the direction of Al Asad [Qadessiya AB]."

The 58th TFS Eagles were subsequently credited with destroying one MiG-29 "Fulcrum" and two Mirage F1EQs.

HORNETS VS "FOXBATS" – JANUARY 17, 1991

By 0340hrs the "Gorillas" and "Tigers" had completed their sweeps and crossed the Saudi border southbound, climbing "through the thirties" to above 40,000ft, heading for Tabuk and Al Kharj. Passing beneath them "in the twenties," headed north, were the US Navy's three strike packages – two SEAD (suppression of enemy air defenses) groups and an "alpha strike" against Tammuz AB. Crossing the frontier between 25,000 and 29,000ft, the "alpha strike" was led by ten F/A-18C Hornets from VFA-81 and VFA-83, from USS *Saratoga* (CV-60), arrayed in a wide "wall" (actually a wide right echelon), with two to five miles between aircraft and each "stacked" 1,000ft above the one ahead to avoid mid-air collisions. The F/A-18s were sweeping the airspace ahead of the strikers and would provide SEAD support for them. Five from VFA-83 "Rampagers" formed the left/west half of the "wall," with five jets from VFA-81 "Sunliners" comprising the east/right half. The Hornets fanned out to arrive at individual HARM launch points that formed a semi-circle around the western side of Tammuz.

The strikers were eight Grumman A-6E Intruders, four (*Saratoga*'s VA-35) dive-bombing from 25,000ft at 0400–0403hrs, each dropping four Mk 84 2,000lb bombs on two large hangars, followed by four (from VA-75, embarked on USS *John F. Kennedy* (CV-67)) hitting the two hardened MiG-29 assembly facilities with 2,000lb GBU-10 LGBs at 0404–0407hrs. They were supported by three EA-6Bs (VAQ-130) escorted by two pairs ("sections") of F-14As (VF-32), all from *Kennedy*. Due to the Tomcats lacking onboard electronic identification (EID) capability, to eliminate the risk of fratricide (also known as "blue on blue" or "friendly fire") to USAF F-15Cs and F-15Es exiting the area, the F-14s were not allowed to sweep ahead of the US Navy strike packages (except for in the far west H3 area). Instead, they were relegated to close escort of the slower and relatively defenseless carrier-based attack and support aircraft.

Because the remaining Iraqi radars had greater range at higher altitudes, the large US Navy strike formation was detected before it had crossed the border, headed northbound. By this time (approximately 0330hrs), the only IrAF fighters still airborne were a pair of MiG-29s attempting to intercept B-52s hitting Talha. Once the Tammuz IOC determined that the largest group of attackers was apparently headed north towards Qadessiya AB (Al Asad), No. 96 Sqn was ordered to scramble a MiG-25PD to intercept the approaching "alpha strike."

Taking the call was Lt Zuhair Dawoud, one of four "Foxbat" pilots "on standby alert in the main aircraft shelter" at Qadessiya. Dawoud later recounted, "At 0238hrs ["Baghdad time"/0338hrs "Riyadh time"] the Air Defense telephone rang and I answered. There was a guy screaming at the other end of the line 'MiG-25 IMMEDIATE TAKEOFF!' So I hurried to the aircraft. In fact, the technicians were ready for this moment, as was the jet, so the takeoff was exceptionally fast – I was airborne just three minutes after I had received the call. After takeoff I switched to safe [secure] frequency and established contact with GCI of the Air Defence Sector. The sky was clear, with very good visibility. The GCI started to give me directions to a group of aircraft that had penetrated Iraqi air space to the south of the base."

A still photograph, from a Soviet training film, showing the *Smerch* K-10T radar display in the target track mode – the target is the bright spot at the base of the upper red vertical line (radar azimuth-and-elevation cross) and the dot in the upper left quadrant is the "steering dot". The circle is called the "allowable steering error" or ASE Circle – when in range, as long as the pilot keeps the "dot in the circle" during the firing sequence, the R-40RT missile could make it to the target. (Tom Cooper Collection)

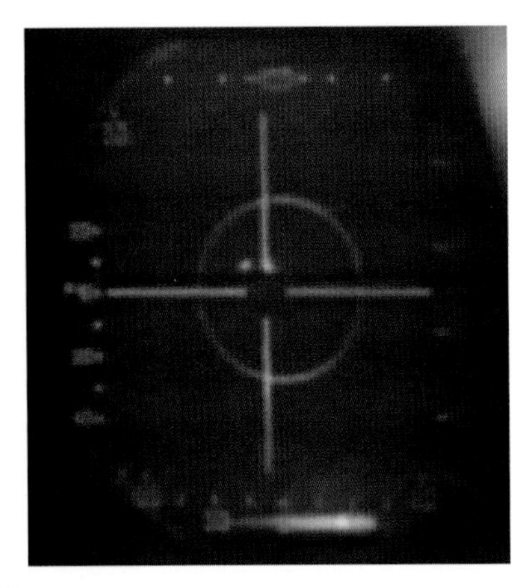

Immediately after takeoff, Dawoud turned south, climbing in full afterburner to 8,000m (26,247ft) and accelerating to Mach 1.4, with his *Smerch-A2* radar in "standby" mode, still warming up. Ahead of him, in the darkness, he was pointed at the center of the phalanx of Hornets, almost directly at the "Sunliners'" boss, Cdr Michael T. "Spock" Anderson.

About 70 miles south of Qadessiya, at 25,000ft, Anderson, flying aircraft "AA401," saw the MiG-25 on his radar. "I got an immediate radar contact on an airborne target climbing out of an airfield [ahead of us]," Anderson subsequently recalled. "I immediately knew it was an enemy airplane because we have some [EID] technology on board the F/A-18. I could see the afterburner flame, and it was an extremely long yellow flame that I had seen before on a MiG-25. There is no question

F/A-18C BuNo 163484 "AA403" from USS *Saratoga* (CV-60) during a deployment to France prior to participating in Operation *Desert Storm*. This aircraft was shot down by a No. 96 Sqn MiG-25PD during the early hours of January 17, 1991. (Jean-Jacques Petit via Tom Cooper)

about what you have when you see that. As soon as I took a radar lock on him, he turned right, and at that point he started to go around me in a counter-clockwise direction. I did a couple of circles with him."

Dawoud confirmed the initial intercept and maneuvering geometry, stating, "My radar was still warming and I was 90km [48.6 miles] from the target formation when an enemy aircraft locked [onto] me with radar. So I performed a hard maneuver and the lock broke."

Despite his positive EID and visual identification (VID), Anderson held his fire while awaiting a confirmation from AWACS. However, the quick-reacting, fast-climbing "Foxbat" had just appeared at the far edge of the Sentry's radar scopes and, without an electronic signature (Dawoud's radar was not transmitting) to correlate with the radar contact, "Cougar" could not confirm the target was hostile. The Hornet and "Foxbat" both turned towards each other, making a complete circle in the darkness – afterburners burning brightly – until passing each other "180-out," then Dawoud rolled out and came out of afterburner, causing Anderson to lose sight of him, and "bugged out" headed almost directly east, roaring over Anderson's wingman, flying "AA406."

Flying "tail end Charlie" in the long, wide echelon was Lt Cdr Scott "Spike" Speicher in "AA403" (BuNo 163484). Approaching his launch point at 364 knots and 28,160ft, he disengaged the autopilot at 03:49:43hrs, selected "burner" and "bunted" over slightly to accelerate for his first HARM launch – recovery of "AA403's" digital storage unit during the 1995 examination of the crash site provided a detailed account of the jet's flight parameters. In 17 seconds Speicher accelerated to 540 knots and descended to 27,872ft.

Dawoud continued his story. "I reported what happened to the GCI and he told me to return to my original intercept course as I had 'targets at 38km [20.5 miles].' Meanwhile, my radar became ready. I locked a target 38km [20.5 miles] from me and at 29km [15.6 miles] I fired [the] R-40RD missile from under my right wing. I kept the target locked with my radar [un]till I witnessed a huge explosion in front of me. I kept looking for the aircraft going down spirally to the ground with fire engulfing it."

At 0350hrs an AWACS controller saw two contacts "merge." The R-40RD detonated, from the left side, beneath the Hornet's cockpit. The explosion of the 154lb high-explosive (HE) blast-fragmentation warhead instantly slewed the aircraft

50–60 degrees right, causing 6G side-forces that sheared off the external fuel tanks and their pylons, as well as one HARM. The pilot ejected, but died later. "AA403" crashed 48 miles due south of Qadessiya.

Dawoud banked right to give the blast a wide berth, and when he rolled back to the left, he could not spot the flaming debris falling earthwards. He did not have much time to look, for almost immediately the Tammuz IOC ordered him to vector south. The second wave of US Navy attack jets was approaching.

Following 48 miles behind Speicher was the CO of VA-75, Cdr Robert Besal, in A-6E "AC504" ("Battleaxe 41"), flown by Lt Cdr Mike "Ziggy" Steinmetz, with his three wingmen in eight-mile trail behind him. Only two minutes after the Hornet was hit, Besal recalls, "There was a call from our AWACS, '"Battleaxe," possible "Foxbat," high, 260 degrees, 60 miles from IKE, heading south.' As I fumbled with my chart to find the IKE reference point, our ALR-67 warning scope lit up with a bright capital letter 'I' – for interceptor. Short seconds later, the bandit appeared.

"He was closing like a bullet from 1:30 high, slicing down toward us, with two large afterburner flames behind him. 'Ziggy' started a right turn as I craned my neck to keep the MiG in sight. As he overshot behind us, 'Ziggy' resumed course, and I hoped that our wingman behind us hadn't closed on us too much. The 'Foxbat' [circled around and then] roared up from our 'six o'clock,' passed us off the left side and zoomed upward, still in 'burner, then pitched over for another run on us. I wondered how much fuel he had, and what the missile would look like as it came off his wing toward us. After a second run with no luck, the MiG blazed away to the northeast, toward Al Taqaddum."

Dawoud's account does not mention the head-on pass, but resumes by describing his stern attack on "Battleaxe 41." "Meanwhile, I locked another target from behind and I asked the GCI for permission to fire but the GCI refused and asked me to confirm the target visually. So I approached it . . . [un]till I reached eight kilometers [4.3 miles] and prepared R-40TD heat-seeking missile and asked the GCI again for permission to fire but he denied my request again so I asked him why? He told me there was a MiG-29 [that] took off ten minutes after me and he lost track with it and he feared I might [be] engaging it. I told him this slow-moving target was impossible to be a MiG-29 but he insisted I disengage and return to base. So I moved past the target aircraft . . . I can still remember [seeing] the cockpit lights of that aircraft.

"I asked the GCI for directions to base because there was a problem with the navigation instruments in my aircraft, and he told me that he had lost radar contact with me! I [had a] feeling of despair as fuel was becoming low and the navigation instruments [were] down, and as it was dark, I could see nothing of ground features as electricity was lost all over the place . . . The only thing I could see was AAA and SAM fire. But suddenly I noticed that Haditha train station had electrical power and since I knew its location [was] 35km [19 nautical miles] north of base, I turned around toward the base and connection with GCI [was] re-established but with very poor quality and he told me to switch to base frequency and I did it, but no one was responding.

"[As] I started approaching the base, I switched the wing lights of the aircraft [on] so they would know it's friendly airplane, and the runway lights were switched on for me. But suddenly, the landing officer was screaming to me, 'DO NOT LAND AT THE MAIN RUNWAY!' So I made a turn and landed in the secondary runway (later

I understood that the main runway was cratered by bombing in its last one-third). No one was there when I landed. All [were] inside shelters. So I taxied the aircraft to the gate of one of the shelters and while doing that I noticed the amount of destruction to the base with concrete chunks and metal objects all over the place. I increased the thrust so they could hear the sound of the engine inside the shelter and let me in – it worked and they let me and the aircraft to go to the shelter."

While Dawoud was airborne, Qadessiya had been attacked by three RAF Tornado GR 1s. By that time other "Foxbats" were taxiing out for takeoff, one of them being badly damaged by the Tornados' JP233 "mines" strewn across taxiways; its pilot was badly injured. None of them took off.

EAGLES VS "FOXBATS" – JANUARY 19, 1991

Overall, IrAF Air Defense units flew 66 "immediate sorties" (interceptor scrambles) on the first day of combat, 37 of them in the western and central sectors, claiming one victory in SOC-West (the F/A-18) and four "kills" in SOC-Center (no Coalition manned aircraft were lost, however). Following that day's disappointing results against the F-15Cs – losing three MiG-29s and two Mirages, with no Eagle "kills" to balance the score sheet – the IrAF only flew 41 sorties the next day while fighter leaders determined a more specific plan for dealing with the Coalition air strikes and their F-15 escorts. Nos. 6 and 39 Sqns' "Fulcrums" would primarily be targeted against Coalition strikers and supporting aircraft while Nos. 96 and 97 Sqns' "Foxbats" were to trap escorting Eagles.

The first opportunity to execute this revised air defense employment plan was on January 19 during the US Navy's midday "alpha strike" against the al-Iskandariyah munitions plant, al-Qa Qaa ammunition plant, and al-Musayyib rocket test facility. The 12 F/A-18 Hornets (VFA-82 and VFA-86 from USS *America* (CV-66)) attacked the first two while eight A-7Es (VA-46 and VA-72 from *Kennedy*) were to strike the latter. Five more A-7Es provided HARM support against SA-3 and SA-6 sites defending the targets, while three EA-6Bs (VAQ-137 from *America*) provided jamming support. Some A-7Es, because of their slower speed and lower maneuvering performance, were provided with close escort in the form of four F-14 Tomcats (from VF-32).

As the attacks occurred, four MiG-29s (No. 39 Sqn) and a Mirage F1EQ scrambled from Qadessiya, followed by two MiG-25s from No. 97 Sqn's detachment deployed the previous day to al-Wallid AB. Maj Koutaiba Sayd led the first pair of "Fulcrums." Climbing to 10,000ft, he was vectored southwards to chase down the US Navy strikers as they departed the target area. Capt Jameel Sayhood led the second pair, and he reported engaging four RAF Tornados at low altitude over Qadessiya and shooting one of them down with an R-60MK "Aphid." No Coalition losses correlate to this claim, however.

Leading the three-ship formation of SEAD Corsairs ("Implant 61") supporting the al-Iskandariyah strike was Lt Cdr Val "VD" Diers, who later recounted, "After the strike, everybody was gone except us. We had 100 knots of headwind and 100nm to the border. I was the target for four MiG-29s and an F1 [launching] out of Al Taqaddum [*sic*]. The F1 went away, but the MiG-29s locked me at 54nm, according

Capt Rick "Kluso" Tollini, who shot down a MiG-25 "Foxbat" with an AIM-7M on January 19, 1991. (Rick Tollini via Author)

to AWACS, and closed to five miles on my tail. We started at 24,000ft and ramped down to 16,000ft for speed, but they still succeeded in running us down.

"The Tomcats [escorting us] stayed on each shoulder doing a fighter weave [to try to pick up the closing "Fulcrums" visually] and I, in frustration, was about to turn solo to engage. I was ready to 'pickle' my drop-tank to engage with [Side]Winder and guns because they had me cold. There was nothing else I could do. The AWACS female controller – I can still hear her today – said 'You have to do something; they're right there!'"

About that time, two formations of F-15Cs locked up the MiG-29s and were closing from the west and southwest to engage. From the west, CAPing for Strike Eagles on "Scud hunting" missions in western Iraq, came "Citgo 21," a four-ship led by Capt Rick "Kluso" Tollini, the 58th TFS weapons officer, who flew an easterly intercept heading to cut off the "Fulcrums." His wingman was Capt Larry "Cherry" Pitts, with Capts John "JB" Kelk and Mark "Willie" Williams as his second element. Tollini later recalled, "We got into a cut-off intercept on the first group [of 'Fulcrums'] from the southwest while they were headed due south from Al Assad or Al Taqaddum airfield, northwest of Baghdad. As we pressed closer, another group appeared about 30 degrees to the left of us and about 60 miles out – both groups closing on us. It looked to me like they were doing some sort of decoy tactic to get us to go after one while the other came in behind us. At 35 miles we locked them [first group] up and they [turned and] started heading east towards Baghdad."

Sensing the situation was becoming critical, "Cougar" had also vectored its HVA CAP ("Citgo 25"), a two-ship led by Capt Cesar "Rico" Rodriguez, with Capt Craig "Mole" Underhill on his wing, to intercept the MiGs as well. When the two formations of Eagles closed to 30 miles – just as Sayd's "Fulcrums" were approaching firing parameters on the fleeing A-7Es – the MiG-29s were alerted by GCI, disengaged, and turned east-northeast, towards Baghdad.

Initially unseen because they were headed almost due west, "hiding" in the AWACS's "Doppler notch," were the two MiG-25s, flown by Capt Sa'ad Nehme and Lt Hussein Abdul Sattar. Recent correspondence from surviving IrAF veterans report that these two MiG-25PD/PDS pilots were flying "Foxbat-Bs," with the assigned task to lead the four-ship of F-15Cs into a "SAM trap." It will be noted, however, that the F-15C pilots visually identified the "Foxbats" as MiG-25PD/PDS interceptor variants by the sighting of four underwing missile pylons, which are not mounted on MiG-25RBs.

As soon as the two MiG-25s turned south, suddenly they appeared on the Americans' radars – with "Cougar" initially calling them out as more "Fulcrums." Tollini recalled, "As we chased [Sayd's 'Fulcrums'] we saw the second group [Nehme's 'Foxbats'] in a 30-mile lead-trail formation with the first group, in a north-south orientation. That made it look like a decoy tactic to me." With the two "Fulcrums" now headed east-northeast at high speed, Tollini turned his four-ship formation due north to face the "Foxbats" – "Citgo 25" continued to chase Sayd's "Fulcrums" and

MiG-25PDS "FOXBAT" COCKPIT

1. Gunsight
2. Cockpit lamps
3. Attitude reference unit
4. Air inlets indicator
5. Distance to waypoint
6. Missile launch/jettison switch
7. Radar control switch
8. Trim control switches
9. Engine warning lights
10. Engine indicator lights
11. RPM indicator
12. Engine temperature indicator
13. Fuel quantity gauge
14. Fuel and systems function lights
15. Cabin temperature indicator
16. Cabin pressure indicator
17. Auto-pilot panel
18. Radar control panel
19. True airspeed/Mach indicator
20. Clock
21. Radio altimeter
22. Pressure altimeter
23. G indicator
24. Artificial horizon
25. Radar screen
26. Combining glass
27. Landing parachute deployment button
28. Armament lower panel
29. Landing gear emergency release handle
30. Fire extinguisher/landing light switch
31. Emergency radio antenna switch
32. Navigation control panel
33. VHF radio channel switch
34. Utility switch panel
35. ARK-43 radio compass control
36. Weapons control switches
37. IFF control panel
38. Engine starting switch
39. Flaps control panel
40. Throttle controls
41. Utility switch panel
42. Control column/weapons firing buttons
43. Rudder pedals
44. Ejection seat
45. Landing gear control lever
46. Landing gear position indicator
47. Vertical speed/slip indicator
48. Indicated airspeed
49. Directional gyro compass
50. Pressure altimeter
51. Ejection seat handles

eventually engaged Sayhood's two-ship. Tollini arrayed his formation in line abreast – a "Wall of Eagles" – with "Citgo 21" (Tollini and Pitts) to the right/east and "Citgo 23" (Kelk and Williams) to the left/west, headed north at 25,000ft altitude, with the two wingmen on the flanks.

As he and Kelk searched for the approaching MiG-25s, Tollini had Pitts continue monitoring Sayd's MiG-29s as they headed towards Baghdad. As Pitts later related, "I was on the far right side of the formation and we had two groups on radar with about a 30-mile azimuth split, so my targeting responsibilities was for the right, or eastern, group [Sayd's 'Fulcrums']. 'Kluso' and 'JB' were putting their radars into this western group ['Foxbats'], and by 25 miles the bandits were maneuvering aggressively. I was splitting my time between the guys that were 'cold' [running away] on the east side, which were my targeting responsibility, and the 'hot' [approaching] western group – I was starting to get nervous that this might be some sort of 'drag' tactic, setting a trap for us, so I wanted to shoot these guys quick before they turned back towards us."

Tollini continues his description. "Once we locked up the 'Foxbats' they also maneuvered – this time to the west – and I remember that as they turned through west to the north, I thought we were going to have to chase them. Fairly quickly, though, they continued a full right 270-degree turn to the south, coming straight at us from 30 miles out in a three- to five-mile lead-trail formation, down around 3,000ft MSL [above mean sea level] – about 2,000ft AGL [above ground level]. Based on my feeling that a trap was being laid for us, and the lead 'Fulcrums' could re-enter our fight, my intention was to shoot a couple of AIM-7s, kill these guys BVR and leave the fight as quick as possible. With the intent of engaging the 'Foxbats' at maximum range, 'JB' and I 'sorted' the targets – I locked the lead 'Foxbat' and 'JB' the trailer – at approximately 30nm, which was almost double the range we would normally lock at.

Capt Larry "Cherry" Pitts also destroyed a MiG-25 "Foxbat" with an AIM-7M on January 19, 1991. (Larry Pitts via Author)

"Because our respective radars were now occupied in a single-target-track mode I wanted to make sure the wingmen ['Cherry' and 'Willie'] were continuing to search for other undetected bandits. As we approached firing range, I directed 'Cherry' and 'Willie' to swap [radar] looks, so 'Cherry' now looked low. With the fight gravitating down low, I wanted his radar down there to assist if needed. I'm glad I did that or it may have turned out differently, because a few moments later the 'Foxbats' did a maneuver to the east that took away our shot capability.

"The two MiG-25s began a 'notch' maneuver to the east at almost the exact moment 'JB' and I were about the fire our AIM-7s. The timing, whether by luck or design, was perfect. The 'Foxbats'' maneuver caused both of our radars to lose lock on them as they 'disappeared' in the ground clutter. Having seen this type of maneuvering so many times in training, I instinctively knew the only thing to do was re-establish a patient radar search pattern down low and at the approximate range I expected Iraqi fighters to exit out of the 'notch.' Sure enough, as we closed to inside 10nm, the two radar targets reappeared on 'Cherry's' and my own radar and we quickly locked the 'Foxbats' at the extreme look-down vertical limits of our radars.

"The 'Foxbats' had 'notched' to the east, across our nose, and then did a right turn 'hot' back to the south – this put them slightly east of me and almost directly under 'Cherry.' As it turned out, I was locked to the leader [Nehme], and made a hard nose-low pull to the right [east] in my final attempt to achieve a pre-merge shot and [get a] 'Tally' on the lead 'Foxbat.' I crossed 'Cherry's' six [o'clock] in doing so. I had no valid shot on the lead 'Foxbat,' but as I looked down I got the 'Tally' on him very low, just above the undercast, and screaming south in a straight line at high speed. I recognized quickly that I did not have much of a chance to get to weapons parameters on the lead 'Foxbat' based on his speed, low altitude, and opening range/velocity. My decision was clarified almost simultaneously as I heard 'Cherry' call 'Engaged!' on the trailing 'Foxbat.' I knew I needed to support 'Cherry's' fight, so I let the leader go."

As Pitts recalled, "I got a radar contact five miles off my nose, going left to right at 500ft and 700 knots! I was at 10,000ft, so I called 'Engaged!' and split-Sed down towards the bandit. 'Kluso' came back with 'Press!,' which set the roles with me as the shooter and 'Kluso' supporting. The bandit was moving so fast that he flew off the right side of my radar scope, and I actually pulled 12Gs and seriously over-stressed the jet! The low cloud deck worked in my favor – it helped me get a 'Tally' on him, and I was able to VID him as a MiG-25. I relocked him with a boresight Auto-Acq mode and he started to break to the right – not that the turn radius of a 'Foxbat' doing 700 knots is very impressive, but he tried. I had no trouble staying inside his circle, and as I ramped down I got to a point 70 degrees to the right side of his tail as he turned through west, at 9,000ft slant range. He was at about 300ft above the undercast. I was a couple of hundred feet above him with a good AIM-9 tone. I uncaged and shot an AIM-9M, but he put out a load of flares that dragged it off.

"As soon as he hit north, he stopped turning and tried to run, still at 300ft and now doing 500 knots. I selected and launched an AIM-7, felt the clunk [as it released] and then looked to the right and saw that it was almost flying in formation with me. The rocket motor then lit and it accelerated off, right at him and passed his canopy without fuzing."

Now 6,000ft behind the "Foxbat," looking right up the tailpipes, Pitts re-selected AIM-9M, got a good tone and uncaged the missile's seeker head. "Just as I was about to fire, he put out more flares that dragged the seeker head off before I could take the shot. I re-caged it back to the radar, got a good tone and shot, but he decoyed it with flares again. He was fighting pretty hard and I was thinking, 'Man, am I going to have to gun this guy?' I selected another AIM-7 and shot, and this time the missile went right up his tailpipe and exploded. The guy bailed out and his ejection seat came right over my canopy – I thought it was going to hit me!" Unfortunately, despite his ejection, Hussein Abdul Sattar was killed.

Tollini followed as the "supporting fighter," later saying, "The last thing I saw of 'Cherry' was him rolling over onto his back and starting a high-G vertical split-S maneuver. 'Cherry's' jet quickly disappeared off my left side, and since I was already in a nose-low rolling right turn, I just continued [to the right], pulling some heavy Gs, and rolled out on a northwest heading, descending to co-altitude with 'Cherry' and his 'Foxbat,' which was now directly off 'Cherry's' nose.

"With 'Cherry' camped out near the 'Foxbat's' 'six o'clock' position I had a perfect

Following a close pass to confirm the first Foxbat was "a dead fighter", "Kluso" Tollini came out of the engagement in a high-G right-hand turn, his radar in the Auto-Guns mode, scanning the airspace ahead of him inside his turn. [Tyson V. Rininger via Steve Davies]

vantage point from about two miles out, looking across the circle from just slightly aft of the 'Foxbat's' 'three o'clock.' It appeared that the 'Foxbat' had shallowed out his turn somewhat, possibly trying to look behind to locate 'Cherry.' He seemed to be in a 2-3G high-speed shallow turn. The first thing I noticed was the 'Foxbat' was putting out a very well-timed stream of chaff, followed by flares, more chaff, more flares, etc. The chaff was so heavy I could see it blossoming as a grayish cloud with each dispense. And the flares came out in long strings of seven to eight each time.

"I knew this was going to be a problem for 'Cherry,' and sure enough I watched as his first AIM-9 'Mike' came off and immediately went after the flares. I then watched his first Sparrow leave the jet but, instead seeing a steady lag-pursuit missile path, the AIM-7 accelerated out front, started to pull lead and then made a high-G turn directly into the ground. Almost immediately I saw Cherry shoot another AIM-9M with the same results as the first, guiding on the 'Foxbat's' flares.

"This entire time as I watched [about 10-12 seconds] I had closed across the circle to about 9,000ft at the 'Foxbat's' 'three o'clock.'. I had my own AIM-9M uncaged and ready to rip. My -9M did not seem to have the same problem with the 'Foxbat's' flares probably because of my beamish approach, and the fact that his flares were not fully blooming until well aft of his jet. The -9M seeker was growling loudly and held steady on the 'Foxbat's' exhaust throughout the engagement. For this reason [and concern that 'Cherry' would run out of missiles] I called out on the radio 'Two, come off!' and a moment later I shot my -9M. Apparently, as he told me afterwards, Cherry never heard my call, possibly because he was calling what would be his final shot over the radio at the same time.

"I watched as his second AIM-7 lumbered off and flew the pursuit path of a Sparrow that had found its target. 'Cherry's' missile reached the target first, and I saw the warhead detonate at the extreme aft end of his tail section, but the MiG kept flying. Within another second or two my AIM-9 arrived, with similar results – an aft end warhead impact with the 'Foxbat' continuing to fly on.

"At this point I heard 'Cherry's' 'Splash!' call. I was now inside 6,000ft on the 'Foxbat' and closing quickly. I never saw the pilot eject, which 'Cherry' would tell me about later, so just to be sure this 'Foxbat' was finished I selected Guns and closed to make a final firing pass. As I did so I noticed the Iraqi fighter rolling out [of its turn] with its previously brightly lit 'burner cans now cold and dark. It was obviously a 'dead' fighter at this point, as I passed very close [inside 500ft] of its tail and watched the 'Foxbat' slowly drift down, almost like a sinking ship, and disappear into the undercast.

"The switch to Guns mode was fortuitous, because my Auto-Guns [auto-acquisition] radar mode broke lock at the extreme right side limits of the radar and started searching for other targets as I made a 600+ knot, high-G turn to the right, through east and back towards the south, intending to egress southwest in the direction I last saw 'Cherry' heading. I didn't know at the time where the other 'Foxbat' was, so I did not want to stick around a merge that was full of missile trails and flares. Also, there would soon be smoke marking the area from the first 'Foxbat's' impact with the ground.

"Somewhere in the middle of 'Cherry' finishing off the 'Foxbat' and me coming around the corner to egress, 'Cougar' had made a high-SA call of 'Threat, south, eight [miles], inbound.' Almost immediately, and simultaneously, 'Cherry' and I both found the returning 'Foxbat.' 'Cherry' used his visual lookout and me my Auto-Guns mode, with my radar and HUD coming to life, showing a target very close, on my nose, moving left to right. Cherry called out, 'Lead, you got one on your nose,' and I thought to myself 'That's right.' Now it was my turn.

"Looking out through the HUD, I quickly acquired a 'Tally-ho,' with the 'Foxbat' directly in front of me about two miles out. He was traveling fast in a northerly straight line moving from left to right, and I approached from his right front quarter [about his 'one' or 'two o'clock']. The line of sight of his flightpath was breaking rapidly to my right, so I recognized the opportunity for a 'lead turn' and I was able to simply continue my high-G right-hand turn and quickly anchor myself at his 'six o'clock,' close to 6,000ft off his tail. Whether the 'Foxbat' pilot saw me or not, it was in the process of my maneuver to the 'Foxbat's 'six o'clock' that he commenced what I might describe as a 'break turn.' Much as 'Cherry's' 'Foxbat,' the extent of his turning ability was probably 3–4Gs."

As Tollini arrived at Nehme's "six o'clock," he could not immediately identify the target. "When we merged the first time we had good ID, but having been spat out of the fight [the 'Foxbat' extending to the south] I didn't know who he was when he came back in again. I didn't know where 'JB' and 'Willie' were, and I knew that there was a Navy package out there somewhere, so I was sitting about a mile behind him, looking at his tail, but unsure of what he was. What I could see was his two huge 'burner plumes, so I asked on the radio, 'Hey is anybody in 'burner?'"

Pitts responded with "Affirm[ative]."

"Based on 'Cherry's' answer, I called, 'Everybody out of 'burner!' – working on the basis that if he was one of us he would comply. Well, he didn't, so I looked at him more closely and saw that he had two missile pylons under each wing. It was not an F-15 or F-14. That's the moment I knew it was a 'Foxbat.' I then started shooting.

"My first AIM-7 was at low aspect, maybe 20 to 30 degrees off the tail, and I hit the pickle button and waited, but I didn't see the missile flying out in front of me. I think the rocket motor failed to light. I thumbed forward [on the HOTAS weapons switch] to select an AIM-9, at which time what looked like a single flare popped out of the aircraft – it was not really bright and it could have been him 'punching out' [ejecting]. In any case, having seen what happened to 'Cherry's' missiles, I was not confident that the AIM-9 would get there, so as soon as I fired it I thumbed back to AIM-7 again. The AIM-9 flew close to his 'burner cans – through the plume – and appeared to fuze, but too far aft, resulting in a miss. I then shot the second AIM-7.

"This time, after a short pause for the launch/motor fire sequence, I saw the Sparrow missile fly out in front of my jet and begin a constant acceleration on a smooth right-hand turn that

In full afterburner, from the stern aspect, the MiG-25 looked much like the F-15 seen in the previous photograph – Tollini had to be sure the target was a "Foxbat" before firing. The four weapons pylons on the wings, and the fact the target stayed in afterburner following his radio call, convinced him that his target was indeed a MiG-25. (USAF)

almost exactly matched the 'Foxbat's' own flightpath. Finally, I saw the missile disappear under the 'Foxbat's' belly. In what seemed to take an eternity, to the point where I again considered making a gun attack, I waited for the warhead to go off. In retrospect, it appeared that the AIM-7 actually impacted the underside of the 'Foxbat,' with the back-up contact fuze finally setting off the Sparrow's large blast-frag warhead. The explosion was huge, like the 'Death Star' from the *Star Wars* film! Unlike the first 'Foxbat,' this one totally disintegrated in a breathtaking flash."

Tollini's main concern had been to end the fight and clear the area as quickly as possible – AWACS was warning that a third group of MiGs [Sayhood's two 'Fulcrums'] had appeared, and there was still a Mirage F1EQ "stooging about" the area trying to get into the fight. Due to the "Foxbat" pilots' effective radar missile defense tactics, and the duration of the high-speed, low-altitude "dogfight" that resulted, Tollini's flight had been involved in a time-consuming, hard-turning engagement in which the pilots were focused exclusively on what was happening inside the "furball." Fortunately, with Kelk and Williams clearing the way, Pitts and Tollini exited the area southwest without any further complications, climbing to meet the tanker that AWACS sent north to meet them.

Nehme survived the engagement, with injuries. As Tollini later related, "Based on our position of advantage, superior weapon systems, and training, it was a bit of a surprise that the Iraqi 'Foxbat' pilots not only survived to the merge, but also performed well enough to prolong the engagement as long as they did. It taught me a valuable lesson to never underestimate your adversary. While it was not the case throughout most of the war, on this day the IrAF came out to fight, and it performed with both courage and determination."

EAGLES VS "FLOGGERS" – JANUARY 26, 1991

Following the defeat on January 19, when USAF F-15Cs claimed six IrAF fighters (two MiG-25s, two MiG-29s, and two F1EQs) without loss, Saddam Hussein "began to lose confidence that Iraqi air defense forces could engage the enemy and live to fight another day." Consequently, he ordered "one of the most important requirements for a long war is to conserve everything." Subsequently, IrAF jets were sequestered in hardened aircraft shelters (HASs) and the pilots "bided their time" until they could again challenge the Coalition air forces.

However, CENTAF was not going to allow the IrAF to just "hunker down" in their bunkers and "ride out the storm." After attacking Iraqi leadership, communications, IADS, and other strategic targets during the first 72 hours of the campaign, followed by three days of bombing nuclear, biological, chemical, and Scud-related installations and facilities, Coalition air forces turned to destroying the IrAF in its lairs. Between January 23 and 27, 16 USAF F-15Es and 40 F-111Fs, US Navy A-6Es and RAF Buccaneers and Tornados used "bunker-busting" LGBs to destroy 375 HASs (of 594 built) and, inside them, 117 IrAF aircraft.

Quite obviously, Saddam Hussein's air force could not survive this one-sided war of attrition. Consequently, on January 26, he decided to safeguard his remaining IrAF aircraft by sending them to Iran, ordering 18 Mirages F1s, nine Sukhoi tactical bombers, and a Dassault Falcon 50 executive jet to "evacuate to Iran immediately." Additionally, he sent a message to his "courageous air falcons" (according to the November 5, 1991 IrAF "Mother of all Battles after action report") explaining that "the enemy's air superiority limited the use of aircraft during battle. For safekeeping, the aircraft have been sent to Iran until the appropriate time to use them against the enemy."

On the night of January 24/25, 20 USAF F-111Fs attacked Jaliba AB with laser-guided 2,000lb GBU-24/BLU-109 "bunker penetrator" bombs, hitting most of the 24 HASs on the airfield. Inside one of them was the No. 96 Sqn detachment of two MiG-25s, both of which were destroyed in their shelter. (USAF)

Due to the range limitations of most Iraqi fighter types, this strategic withdrawal would be conducted in two phases. First, flyable aircraft were withdrawn from outlying bases to those within the "Baghdad Super-MEZ" (Missile Engagement Zone, which boasted the highest concentration of SAMs in Iraq). Movement began that day with the departure of No. 73 Sqn's eight MiG-23MLs from Sa'ad AB for al-Bakr AB. By this time SOC-West, based at al-Wallid, had been destroyed (January 19) and the last surviving IOC disabled (January 21). Consequently, the two four-ship formations, launched about 20 minutes apart and flying extremely low, had no GCI information whatsoever.

The lack of airborne opposition for the past six days resulted in F-15C flights covering Coalition air operations from HVA CAPs near the Saudi border. Mid-afternoon, the 58th TFS "Citgo 25" flight – a four-ship led by Capt Rhory "Hoser" Draeger (59th TFS weapons officer attached to the "Gorillas" for *Desert Storm*) – was patrolling approximately 30 miles south-southeast of Talha airfield. Draeger's wingman was Capt Tony "Kimo" Schiavi, with Capts Cesar "Rico" Rodriguez and Bruce "Roto" Till ("Citgo 27") as his second element.

Draeger (who, sadly, was killed in an automobile accident in March 1995) provided the following account to the USAF Historical Research Agency (AFHRA) for its Gulf War Air Power Survey, document NA-399, "Wall of Eagles – Aerial Engagements and Victories in Operation *Desert Storm*," compiled by John M. Deur. "I had just gotten back [from the tanker] when AWACS said there were bandits airborne from H2 airfield heading east-northeast. I told AWACS that we were committed [on those targets]. We ran basically all the way up to Al Asad airfield. We still hadn't gotten any contacts [the MiG-23s were flying perpendicular to 'Citgo's' intercept heading, concealed in 'the Doppler notch'], and they were probably still 80 miles on our nose. It was a poor intercept heading to begin with, but I kept saying 'Let's give it a chance. Nothing else is going on, so we might as well try to run these guys down or, at least, chase them and find out what's going on.'

"When we got about 15 miles south of Al Asad airfield, AWACS again said that there were multiple bandits taking off from H2 and headed northeast. Well, it seemed like they were following the same track as the other guys, but these were now on a

Three members of "Citgo" Flight relaxing at Tabuk AB. They are, from left to right, Bruce "Roto" Till, Tony "Kimo" Schiavi, and their leader, Rhory "Hoser" Draeger. (Tony Schiavi via Steve Davies)

perfect intercept heading for us. I turned the formation to the west and pushed it up. We were about 80 miles away when we turned to them, and we closed from 80 miles down to 40 miles relatively quickly. I mentioned to the guys [in my flight] that I didn't want them to lock the MiGs up and trigger their RWR. AWACS continued to tell us their heading and I made some small corrections to get a better intercept on them – the final intercept heading ended up being 300 degrees. At 40 miles we began to detect that there were four of them, but at about 35 miles one of them spun off and headed back to the airfield. Right around 28 miles we got a real good break-out on our radar scopes of three of them flying in a[n inverted] vic formation, with the 'stinger' back to the west – we had two guys looking like they were line abreast, and one guy [trailing] in a stinger formation."

The MiG-23MLs were led by Maj Shaker Rehan Hamood, with Capts Karim Hassan Rahel and Amer Hassan on his wings, his third wingman having aborted and returned to Sa'ad AB with a mechanical problem. The Eagles bore down on the "Floggers" in a "wall formation," with "Citgo 25" (Draeger and Schiavi) to the right/north, "Citgo 27" (Rodriguez and Till) to the left/south, with the wingmen on the flanks. The two adversary formations closed with each other almost head-on, with the F-15Cs approaching from the MiGs' "one o'clock" at 1.2 Mach, some 25,000 ft above them – well above the "Floggers'" radar scan.

Draeger continued, "I targeted myself on the leader in the north, I targeted No 2 [Schiavi] on the trailer to the west and I targeted Nos. 3 and 4 [Rodriguez and Till] together on the one to the south. That's a little non-standard for F-15s, but my philosophy has always been that I'm going to shoot the leader and let the other guys in the formation shoot the trailers, so that's the way I [assigned] the targets. Everybody took the correct locks at 18 miles and we shot very shortly after that. I shot first, followed by Nos. 2, 4, and then 3.

"We were up at about 25,000–28,000ft. There was a pretty significant cloud deck underneath us – it wasn't really thick, but we couldn't see the ground either. We were about ten miles from the MiGs when a big hole in the clouds appeared. It ended up being perfect. We dove through that on top of these three MiGs flying along a dirt road in between H2 and H1 airfields.

"My first missile hit the back end of the lead MiG-23 and basically ripped it off the aircraft. I thought for sure he was in the dirt. They were all flying really low, at about 200ft or so, maybe even lower than that. Dirt kicked up on the aircraft, and I thought he went in [crashed]. On my tape, I even said, 'Splash 1 from 1,' but he kept on flying. The MiG-23 doesn't have any fuel flash [fire] suppression – it's just steel against gas. I could see the fire burning up toward his wing root as I was converting on him [for a follow-up AIM-9 shot], and as soon as it hit that internal gas, there was a massive explosion. Everyone diverted their attention to him because it was such a huge fireball – it was probably full of gas at that particular time. He ended up doing about a quarter roll into the dirt."

No. 73 Sqn's Maj Shaker Rehan Hamood, who was killed when his MiG-23ML was downed by "Citgo" Flight on January 26, 1991. (Ali Tobchi via Tom Cooper Collection)

F-15C EAGLE COCKPIT

1. Heads Up Display (HUD)
2. Lock-Shoot lights
3. Air-to-air receptacle "Ready" light
4. Magnetic compass
5. Auxiliary UHF control panel
6. IFF controls and interrogation panels
7. Throttles
8. Radar control panel
9. Fuel control panel
10. ILS/TACAN control panel
11. Landing gear lever and lights
12. Armament control MPCD
13. Fire warning and extinguisher panel
14. Vertical situation (radar) display
15. Mode 3/A IFF control
16. Main UHF control panel
17. HUD control panel
18. Tactical Electronic Warfare Systems (TEWS) display
19. Countermeasures Dispenser (CMD) lights
20. Airspeed/Mach indicator
21. Attitude director indicator
22. Altimeter
23. Angle-of-attack and g meters
24. Horizontal situation indicator
25. Standby flight instruments
26. Vertical velocity indicator
27. Clock
28. Primary engine instruments
29. Hydraulic pressure indicators
30. Fuel quantity indicators
31. Jet fuel starter handle
32. Cabin pressurization altimeter
33. Caution lights panel
34. Oxygen regulator
35. Engine control panel
36. Environmental control system
37. Inertial navigation system controls
38. Cockpit interior lighting controls
39. TEWS control panel
40. CMD control panel
41. Compass control panel
42. Cockpit utility lights
43. Oxygen hose/communications chord
44. Map case
45. Emergency canopy jettison
46. ACES II ejection seat handgrips
47. Control column
48. Pilot's seat
49. Emergency landing gear handle
50. Rudder pedals

USAF F-15C Eagle 85-0104 was flown by Capt Tony "Kimo" Schiavi during the January 26, 1991 engagement with MiG-23MLs of No. 73 Sqn. (Ted Carlson via Steve Davies)

Schiavi recounted his role, starting with the targeting plan, stating, "We got our MiG-23 EID and AWACS clearances out of the way well before we could shoot. The MiGs were at 500ft and, at about 40 miles, 'Hoser' called the targeting plan – he targeted me on the northern [western] trailer and 'Rico' and 'Roto' on the other trailer to the south. Up until now, things had been very calm. You'd almost have thought that we were flying a training mission over the Gulf of Mexico at our home base in Florida. 'Hoser' shot an AIM-7 first, but his missile had a motor no-fire. He shot again and the second Sparrow headed towards the lead 'Flogger.' By now we were calling 'Tally-ho' on the MiGs, and we saw 'Hoser's' missile hit the back end of the airplane. There was this little explosion and a dust cloud, but 'Hoser' called, 'Splash 1 from 1.'

"You could tell that the adrenalin was now pumping because as soon as airplanes started blowing up, everyone's voices went up about six octaves! I fired about seven or eight seconds after 'Hoser,' and I used two missiles because I was coming in at an angle and the guy was low. I also wanted to be sure that the MiG died. We came down very fast through some clouds and moist air, so we were trailing condensation and wingtip streamers pretty good. The MiG pilots saw this and began a hard right-hand turn into us. At that instant my first missile hit the front of the second MiG and it basically vaporised him. My second missile went right through the fireball."

Beginning with the targeting plan, Rodriguez related his role, recalling, "As we sorted the formation, the targeting plan was for Rhory to target the leader, 'Kimo' would target the northern arm and 'Roto' and I would target the southern arm. As we neared weapons employment range, I started to hear shots being taken. Rhory shot first at the leader, and his missile appeared to hit the fuselage, perhaps even go down the intake. Either way, it did not detonate. The missile trashed the entire engine, and as that pilot felt the impact, he started an easy left turn to the north. In the turn the entire MiG-23 aircraft became engulfed in flames as the missile damage became pretty evident.

"The two wingmen checked away from their leader, making a right turn to the southeast. This was directly at us, and it shortened the distance for the missiles that we already had in the air towards them. 'Kimo' had a missile on the northern guy, and 'Roto' and I both had a missile on the southern."

Till's first AIM-7 "hung" on the rail, while the motor in the second missile failed to fire. His third arrived at the target 1.2 seconds after Rodriguez's AIM-7M hit the

"Citgo" Flight's targets were three MiG-23MLs from No. 73 Sqn, similar to these examples, serial numbers 23270 and 23282, that were found derelict at al-Bakr AB in 2003. (USAF)

"Flogger."

Rodriguez continued, "Shortly thereafter, at about seven miles away, I observed 'Kimo's' missile impact his MiG and disintegrate it as my missile-to-MiG merge occurred. The destruction was so complete that, when 'Roto's' missile arrived, there was not enough airplane left for it to fuze against. His missile continued on across the desert floor for some time before it tumbled. In a matter of just a few seconds there was a large smear of fire on the north side of the road where 'Kimo's' MiG remains had impacted, and there was a matching fire smear to the south where my MiG had hit. Rhory had pursued his MiG to the north and had an uncaged AIM-9 ready to employ when his MiG finally exploded. None of the MiG pilots managed to eject."

Hamood and Rahel were killed in the crashes of their "Floggers". Reportedly, according to a surviving IrAF MiG-23 pilot, Capt Amer Hassan "outran the missiles fired at him [one hit the ground behind his aircraft], escaped, survived, and reached al-Bakr unscathed, where he told the sad story of that flight."

EAGLES VS "FLOGGERS" – JANUARY 27, 1991

On January 26 the exodus of IrAF combat aircraft to Iran began, with 23 fighters and attack jets joining the 22 Il-76 transports and support aircraft (as well as five Iraqi and six captured Kuwaiti airliners) that had been ferried to their neighbor during the first two weeks of the air campaign. Withdrawal of combat jets from the outlying bases into the "Super-MEZ" continued the next day, with three MiG-23BNs (No. 49 Sqn) and one F1EQ/BQ, believed to have taken off from Ali Ibn Abu Talib AB (Tallil), attempting to relocate to al-Bakr at midday.

The two very tightly formating two-ships initially headed east, towards Iran, concealed within the "Doppler notch" until north of Basra, where they turned northeast and were spotted by the eastern AWACS (Callsign "Bulldog"). By this time SOC-South, the IrAF's only non-hardened control center (at Abu Talib), had been destroyed (January 18), but along the eastern frontier, the al-Amara IOC was once again operational following damaging attacks (January 20).

OVERLEAF
Looking forward from the cockpit of his F-15C Eagle, Capt Jay "OP" Denney said that, due to their sand-colored camouflage, "We could see the shadows of the 'bandits' better than the aircraft as they descended to 100ft. While [looking back from] checking 'Coma's' 'six' [o'clock], I noticed I was still locked to the first 'bandit' – he had flown out of the [AIM-7] fireball – and he was in a gentle left-hand turn about two miles in front of me. So I uncaged an AIM-9 and fired. This time I watched as the aircraft erupted like a Molotov cocktail across the flat desert terrain." Denney was the only Eagle pilot to achieve his MiG kills using the AIM-9M Sidewinder heat-seeking missile. In the background, Capt Dean "Coma" Powell's two AIM-7Ms streak towards their targets – a MiG-23BN and Mirage F1EQ.

BT
AF
84
025

A two-ship of 53rd TFS "Tigers" – "Opec 01," led by one of the 36th TFW's weapons officers, Capt Jay "OP" Denney – was manning a roving CAP (a 50nm x 100nm "kill box") approximately 60 miles south of Baghdad. On Denney's wing was Capt Dean "Coma" Powell. At about 1055hrs, "Bulldog" called out "bogeys" (unidentified aircraft) using "bullseye" code "Pepsi [Salman Pak airfield], 130 [degrees] for 80 [miles]."

Denney later related, "Putting it together off the bullseye point, I turned my flight east and called for 'bogey dope' from AWACS just for us. 'Bulldog' came back with 'Opec 01, snap [vector] 090 degrees for 85 miles.' We were in the 32–34[,000ft] block, and stroked min[imum] afterburner to hit the Mach. I had 'Coma' on my north [left] side and the sun was high to the south. The bogeys were low – in the 5,000ft regime – headed northwest at 350 knots, and we were getting 'hits' only since they were in an almost perfect beam to us due to geometry. I 'hammered down' [pressed the AAI button] for the ID – no friendlies in the area. We closed on the group. At approximately 20 miles the bogeys turned to the northeast."

According to USAF Intelligence, the al-Amara IOC warned the formation that the Eagles were closing from the west, resulting in the evasive turn to the northeast. This turn caused the formation to split, with the leaders (to the northeast) being followed by the second (western) group about two to three miles in trail. At this point a USAF EC-130H "Compass Call" electronic warfare platform (from the 41st Electronic Combat Squadron) began jamming al-Amara's transmissions, denying the formation any further information.

Denney recalled, "We stayed up at 30,000ft at Mach 1.1 in full afterburner, trying to get closure before they crossed the [Iranian] border. As they turned northeast, I told 'Coma' to 'Break lock and don't spike them' because I didn't want to give them notice that we were chasing them down. Meanwhile, 'Bulldog' called 'Bandit, bandit, cleared to fire' and we armed 'hot' [Master Arm switch to ARM]. I re-sanitized the low block and, with great discipline, 'Coma' reset his radar [altitude] coverage and sanitized high [making sure there were no other bandits in the area].

Capt Jay "OP" Denney was the first F-15C pilot to successfully use the Raytheon AIM-9M Sidewinder heat-seeking missile in combat. An example of the weapon is seen here being loaded onto the Eagle's "missile rail" by 53rd TFS weapons troops. (Jay Denney via Author)

"Opec 01" flight photographed from their tanker shortly after their dramatic engagement with four IrAF fighter-bombers on January 27. (Jay Denney via Author)

"At this point we started getting [a] break-out on them – we still thought there was only two of them. We got to within 15 miles when they made a [left] turn back towards Baghdad, giving us a geometry cut-off. The first contact to turn was the western one, and the eastern one trailed in a four-mile echelon formation to the southeast [of the new leader]. We were now supersonic, ramping down out of the '30s,' clear of SAM zones and closing as we made a lead pursuit turn to 350-degree heading. We had two contacts, in azimuth [side-side break-out] on our VSDs. My flight was northbound, with 'Coma' on my western [left] side, slung slightly aft and high, about 2.5 miles out. We were doing about 600 to 650 [knots] and these guys were only doing about 350 [knots]. I was six miles in trail of the closest [southeast] contact and 'Coma' was about eight to nine miles in trail with his group [northwestern].

"With our 250+ knots of closure, our weapons displays indicated we were in range for AIM-7 shots. I fired first from an altitude of 16,000ft [MSL] at my target, which was at about 300ft [AGL]. The missile came off, guided, and appeared to impact, but he flew out of the blast pattern. He knew it was there because it was right on top of him, and he started a 2–3G left-hand turn. I closed in and followed up with an AIM-9. It was a hit right through his canopy.

"Opec 01" Flight's targets were three MiG-23BNs from No. 49 Sqn (plus a Mirage F1EQ), similar to this example, serial number 23173. The "Flogger-H" ground-attack variant was not popular with the IrAF, equipping only two units, Nos. 29 and 49 Sqns, with only the latter still operational in 1991. (Albert Grandolini Collection)

ENGAGING THE ENEMY

Once the Eagle pilot had successfully closed into weapons employment range and brought the target into the HUD field-of-view, he selected the appropriate weapon and maneuvred into the weapons engagement zone. In this case – using Capt Denney's attack on the "Floggers" on January 27, 1991 (see Battlescene) as an example – the pilot has closed to about 1.1 miles at the target's "six o'clock," prompting the MiG-23 pilot to initiate a defensive turn to the left.

The F-15C is in the "heart of the envelope" for short-range missile (SRM)/AIM-9M employment with 350 knots of overtake. The MiG is in the radar-positioned target designator (TD) "box," with the SRM "seeker circle" uncaged and tracking the MiG's afterburner plume. Beneath the TD box is the SRM triangle "shoot cue." The illuminated (flashing) amber "lock-shoot" lights on the canopy bow emphasize the fact that all weapons parameters are met – all the pilot has to do is push the weapons release ("pickle") button atop the control stick grip.

In this case, one AIM-9M is in flight towards the MiG-23, and a second missile is ready to fire in case the first fails to destroy the target. The last "Flogger" attacked in this engagement can just be seen to the right side of the HUD, fleeing at high speed towards Salman Pak airfield in the distance.

"'Coma' fired immediately after, and while checking 'Coma's' 'six [o'clock]' I watched his first missile trail northward – it just never made it."

Powell picks up the story. "We both took stern AIM-7 shots, and I watched my missile track as long as I could. It was looking good until the rocket motor burned out and I lost sight of it. But both shots missed. [So] I rolled over and did a 'half split-S' and, as I pulled the bandits into the HUD, I could see their formation. They were right on the deck, maybe 100ft [AGL], and as I finished my 'split-S' and started to level off about two miles behind this group I could now see that there were two aircraft.

Denney (left) and Powell pose for the USAF photographer following their successful January 27 engagement. (USAF)

"I'd gotten down to about 3,000ft [MSL], and I could see two jets in my TD [target designator] box. They were so close they looked like they were in 'fingertip' formation – the one on the right was a MiG-23 and the one on the left was a Mirage F1 [EQ]. I put some G on the jet [to ensure the next missiles cleared the external fuel tanks] and fired twice. I watched the missiles track, and it appeared to me that the first AIM-7 drove right up the tailpipe of the F1. He just disintegrated in a huge fireball. The second AIM-7 drove right up on the left wingtip of the 'Flogger.' The missile fuzed, then I saw secondary explosions on the fuselage of the MiG-23, at which point he nosed over and flew into the ground."

From the east, Denney witnessed the destruction of the two Iraqi fighter-bombers. "By now 'Coma' had rolled and pulled his nose down towards the bandits, re-locked, and fired two more AIM-7s. As he locked he called 'Tally 2,' since he had a two-ship that was in welded wing/fingertip formation – a MiG-23 and a Mirage F1. I scanned from his group to the northeast and picked up a fourth bandit about four miles [away] at 'right one o'clock.' 'Coma's' first missile hit his first bandit and the Mirage exploded and cartwheeled across the desert floor about 4,000ft to my left side as I passed it. I saw the 'chute of that pilot at about 200ft above his fireball. I then saw the fourth bandit turning west, bringing his nose toward 'Coma.' His second bandit then exploded when it was hit by the second AIM-7.

"I was at 300ft and 500 knots rolling in on the last MiG. I could not get a boresight [radar] lock, so I uncaged an AIM-9M and got a perfect screaming tone. I fired a no-lock shot from 8,000ft aft. As soon as I fired he reversed his turn back to the right, and the missile appeared to go right up his tailpipe. I had called for 'Coma' to break right when it looked like the MiG 'might' have been turning on him – he was now directly over the top of us, and I was 4,000ft aft of the MiG and climbing as he exploded."

From Powell's vantage point, "I watched 'OP' hose this guy with an AIM-9, and that pilot ejected right away. I'm watching him in his 'chute about 6,000ft off my nose, and I knew this was too good not to do something with. While I knew I couldn't shoot him, what I did was to fly as close to him as I could, in full afterburner, in a high-G turn around him. When he got back to his bar that night, I didn't want there to be any doubt about what got him!"

Finally, Denney added, "We had been closing in towards Salman Pak East, an airfield with a large array of SA-2 SAMs. It seemed like the moment the last MiG went down our RWR erupted with SA-2 spikes! We continued a hard right turn to the southeast, stroked our afterburners, jettisoned our wing fuel tanks and started climbing out towards the south."

OPERATION *SAMURRÁ* – JANUARY 30, 1991

By January 28 some 82 of Iraq's newest and most advanced combat aircraft – including four MiG-29s, 24 Mirage F1s, and 24 Sukhoi Su-24 twin-jet tactical bombers – had been evacuated to Iran. One that did not make it that day was a MiG-23 credited to 32nd TFS Capt Don "Muddy" Watrous from the Incirik-based "War Dogs," the jet being shot down only four miles from the Iranian border – three others got away. The next day another "Flogger" was claimed while fleeing to Iran, this one by 60th TFS pilot Capt David "Logger" Rose, attached to the "Gorillas."

The IrAF's MiG-25 squadrons were not included in this evacuation. Having lost 20 of their original 35 aircraft – 18 destroyed in their HASs and two in air combat – the surviving 15 "Foxbats" remaining at Tammuz and Qadessiya were to be involved in the IrAF's last attempt at engaging the American F-15Cs. In fact, the planning of Operation *Samurrá* began around January 18, bolstered by a successful nocturnal intercept the next night that, although it failed to shoot down any of the EF-111As that were attacked, drove away the airborne jammers and "unmasked" the F-15Es attacking al-Qa'im WMD (Weapons of Mass Destruction) facility. One of the Strike Eagles was subsequently lost to SA-2E SAMs fired by the 147th Air Defense Brigade.

With the failure of the traditional "lead-around" tactic that same day – resulting in the loss of two "Foxbats" to Tollini and Pitts (of the 58th TFS) – a new tactic was devised. In this case, when the opportunity presented itself, two MiG-25s would be vectored individually from different directions against a single, isolated target group – hopefully a two-ship of F-15C Eagles. If the latter stayed together and turned to engage, or defend against, one attacking "Foxbat," the other would be in a flanking position from which to attack, with increased chances for success.

Meanwhile, due to the recent Iran–Iraq War, initially the Iraqi evacuation flights surprised and puzzled CENTAF leaders. Once it was realized that these did not represent "mass defections" but a concerted effort to preserve the IrAF, CENTAF planners established five "barrier CAPs" ("BARCAPs") around Baghdad – two to the west and three to the east – manning them around-the-clock with four-ships of F-15Cs (with one pair "on station" and the other cycling to the tankers for fuel). Watching this operation develop with their surviving radar, the 1st ADS (SOC-Center, now operating from the Taji IOC) saw the opportunity to strike at one of these five relatively isolated F-15 formations – initially planning to launch the mission on January 28, but it was "aborted for several reasons."

Finally, just after noon on January 30, an Iraqi electronic and signals intelligence unit (with the cover designation of "Measurement Unit 128") monitoring AWACS/F-15C radio frequencies reported to the Alternate ADOC at al-Bakr AB that "Xerex 31" – a four-ship of 53rd TFS "Tigers" manning the "Cindy BARCAP" – was approaching "bingo fuel," necessitating the cycling of one two-ship to the tanker. Leaving "Xerex 33" – Capt Tom "Vegas" Dietz and wingman 1Lt Bob "Gigs" Hehemann – in the 30-mile counter-clockwise orbit, Lt Col Randy "Bigs" Bigum and wingman 1Lt Lynn "Boo Boo" Broome headed south to refuel. Because "Cindy CAP" was wedged between the "Baghdad Super-MEZ" and the Iranian border, transiting to and from required threading the channel between them on the hour-and-a-half round-trip to the tanker.

Recognizing the opportunity to implement Operation *Samurrá*, two MiG-25s were ordered off – Capt Mahmoud Awad (No. 96 Sqn) took off from Qadessiya and Capt Mohammed Jassim as-Sammarai (No. 97 Sqn) launched from Tammuz, both climbing to 13,000m (42,650ft). Initially, the two were vectored independently, Awad from overhead Samarra and as-Sammarai via Jisr Diyala (a southern suburb of Baghdad) against what proved to be a spurious radar target over Khan Bani Sa'ad (about 13.5 miles east of Taji). As the "Foxbat" pincer attack closed on the electronic phantom – a pulse radar anomaly most likely caused by a temperature inversion in the upper atmosphere – as-Sammarai fired an R-40RD missile and said he saw it detonate, but "never saw the target, no trace of smoke and no debris."

The effect of this miscue was that the two "Foxbats" came together near Khan Bani Sa'ad and turned west, while their actual targets – "Xerex 33" – were still 40 miles to the east. Additionally, by this time "Xerex 31" flight was on its return from the tanker, being some 80 miles south of Baghdad and headed back to the "Cindy CAP." The Eagles' AWACS – "Bulldog" – had initially called out the "bandits," but soon added, "Skip it, skip it. Bogus targets" when the "Foxbats" faded within the "Baghdad Super-MEZ."

As the Iraqi GCI's "radar picture" cleared, the two MiG-25s were vectored 090 degrees and ordered to engage "Xerex 33" flight, which was patrolling "Cindy CAP" at 35,000ft and about 300 knots to conserve fuel. As the two MiGs completed their turns, as-Sammarai became the leader, with Awad in eight-mile trail. Once the "Foxbats" turned "hot," "Bulldog" called them out to Dietz and Hehemann, saying "Bandits,

No. 97 Sqn MiG-25 pilot Capt Mohammed Jassim as-Sammarai flew the lead jet (serial number 25221) during Operation *Samurrá*. (Ali Tobchi via Tom Cooper Collection)

west, 70 miles. High. Fast." Dietz ordered his formation to turn west and accelerate.

Hehemann later recalled, "I picked them up first with the high look on my radar, I had the leader at about 43,000ft doing 1,020 knots true airspeed – about 1.8 Mach. 'Vegas' called for us to 'push it up' and told me – which was unusual for us – to engage the leader, since I was already locked to him, and he was going to engage the trailer. We complied with the rules of engagement and determined that they were definitely hostile and we were cleared to fire. I 'pickled' the first missile and it actually fell off the airplane – the rocket motor didn't light. Soon after that they fired a missile at us. We both had [RWR] indications that their radars were locked to us, so I followed that first missile up with a second [AIM-7], and it was guiding on the leader. So I maneuvered my airplane to the south, only to look up and determine that I didn't have 'Vegas' in sight – so I called 'Blind.' I was surprised when he called, 'One's blind' – that wasn't the best place to start an engagement. In any case, the leader went into a turn immediately, a left turn through north [and outran the missile]."

At 43,000ft, the curvature of the earth meant that the horizon was about six degrees below level flight, allowing a limited depressed angle for a pulse radar to detect and track a target at a slightly lower altitude, permitting as-Sammarai to lock onto Hehemann. The MiG-25 pilot called out a visual contact and fired an R-40RD at 12 miles. According to Iraqi sources, "As the missile thundered towards them, the F-15s split, the missile going for the left Eagle, going off below it and causing damage to the left engine of the USAF fighter." In reality, as-Sammarai's early turn away from the Eagles had broken the radar lock and the missile went ballistic.

Heheman resumed his account. "'Vegas,' in fact, had crossed underneath me and was coming now to engage the trailer [Awad]. He 'pickled' a few missiles and there were some problems with those – the first one fell off [motor no fire], the second hung on the airplane and the third one fell off too. He was 'spiked' again by the trailer, so he decided it was time to defend himself – he had indications that there was an attack coming toward him, so he did a defensive maneuver to the north and eventually turned 'cold.' He directed us to 'bug out' to the east."

Hehemann had reversed his turn to the right as as-Sammarai turned north to keep his radar tracking the "Foxbat" as it made the wide, high-speed turn back to the west. "Well, I was now coming into a WEZ on the leader, who I now had in sight, and I was inside his turn – he was now heading west. I fired a follow-up missile that guided on him.

"About that time I was 'spiked' by the trailer. He was due west of me, 'left nine o'clock close,' so I was doing the math on how far these two guys were apart and how far I was behind the leader, and determined that I was probably right in the 'heart of the envelope' of every missile the trailer was carrying on his airplane. So I dropped chaff and flares out of my airplane to try to defeat any ordnance the trailer had coming at me. By the time my computer told me that my missile [had] 'timed out,' the leader was still flying and he had accelerated back out to about 1,000 knots. I waited a few more seconds and then lit the 'burners and came off to the east, never having found the trailer, but my 'spike' had dropped – apparently he lost radar contact on me. I was in a 'steep defend' [descending defensive maneuver] down to about 20,000ft, and then ran east with 'Vegas.'"

Meanwhile, watching on radar as the "Foxbats" headed west towards Tammuz, Bigum decided that his two-ship could possibly cut them off, and he turned "Xerex 31" northwest. He had hoped to skirt the "Baghdad Super-MEZ" to the south, but a high-altitude crosswind of 140 knots blew the two Eagles across the Iraqi capital and into a 30-mile trail with the descending MiG-25s. Flying across the top of the "Baghdad Super-MEZ," the F-15Cs were "lit up" by numerous SA-2 and SA-3 RWR indications, but no SAMs were fired – probably to prevent shooting the "Foxbats" instead. Arriving almost overhead Tammuz, Awad and as-Sammarai chopped their throttles to idle, rolled over and performed a "split-S," slowing from 1,000 knots to 300 knots as they literally "dropped" into the landing pattern at Tammuz. The Eagles followed, descending to 20,000ft. The "Foxbat" decelerations allowed them to close to 20 miles as the MiG-25s circled northwest of the airfield to land to the southeast.

"Xerex 31" sorted their targets, with Bigum locked to the leader (Awad) and Broome to the trailer. The latter shot two AIM-7Ms, neither of which hit their target. Approaching within ten miles of the airfield, and descending through 8,000ft, Bigum fired one AIM-7M at Awad, but this MiG-25 landed before the missile arrived. Bigum quickly shifted his radar to as-Sammarai, who had slowed on "short final," and fired another Sparrow. As the MiG-25 touched down and decelerated through 75 knots, the APG-63 lost its lock and the final missile impacted the runway about ten feet off the "Foxbat's" left wingtip.

Breaking left, Bigum and Broome exited the airfield's MEZ to the south before the SAMs could start firing. Back at Tammuz AB, the Iraqis thought that the "Foxbats" had been chased by F-15Es firing AGM-65 Maverick air-to-ground missiles at them. The IrAF credited as-Sammarai with a "possible victory," later upgrading it to "confirmed" on the word of a Bedouin smuggler who reported in mid-summer 1991 to have discovered the wreckage of an F-15 "very close to the coordinates at which our radars lost track of the falling F-15 on January 30."

"Xerex 31" flight, which consisted of 1Lt Bob Hehemann, Capt Tom Dietz, Lt Col Randy Bigum, and 1Lt Lynn Broome. Fortunately for all six pilots involved in the January 30 Eagles versus "Foxbats" engagement, none of the missiles fired connected with their targets. (Bob Hehemann via Steve Davies)

STATISTICS AND ANALYSIS

The "duel" between F-15Cs and MiG-23s and MiG-25s provides a very small sample size for any thorough statistical analysis. However, the overwhelming success of the Eagle, in the hands of well-trained and aggressive USAF fighter pilots – credited with two "Foxbats" and eight "Floggers," as well as five MiG-29s, destroyed without loss – established an unprecedented dominance (a "kill ratio" of 15-to-0 against adversary air-to-air fighters) in the history of air superiority. Nevertheless, while this premier fourth-generation jet fighter was ultimately supreme in the skies over Iraq in 1991, its weapons proved to be less than impressive.

The AIM-7M Sparrow – a legacy weapon from the Vietnam War – was particularly disappointing. USAF F-15C pilots fired 31 AIM-7s to destroy eight "Foxbats" and "Floggers", resulting in a Pk of only 25.8 percent, well short of the theoretical 36-45 percent. More than one third of the failures were "rocket motor no fires" due to breakdowns in the complicated and unwieldy launching sequence that first jettisoned the weapon so that a "lanyard" could be pulled to ignite the rocket motor, then the missile trundled off after its target . . . sometimes.

Four AIM-9M Sidewinders were used to achieve two kills, a Pk of 50 percent, also well below expectations. In this case, the improved AIM-9M's touted "flare rejection capability" proved to be less than advertised. This was because the designers assumed Soviet IR countermeasures (IRCM) would be like American ones – flaring quickly to temperatures much higher than that of the jet exhaust, even in afterburner, so that they would attract the heat-seeking missile away from the cooler-burning engine. So, in layman's terms, the AIM-9M's guidance logic was designed to reject the hotter heat source and home on the cooler one, thus ignoring the IRCM flares. The problem was that due to various design and manufacturing deficiencies, Soviet-made flares ignited more slowly and burned at lower temperatures than their jet engine exhausts when in afterburner. Consequently, the Sidewinder, as designed, went after the cooler heat source – the flares.

The IrAF experienced similar difficulties with their Soviet-made missiles, especially the R-40. There were five known firing attempts – at an F/A-18C, an EF-111A, and an F-15 – of which only one was successful. Three missed due to jamming and one due to tactical considerations, resulting in an overall Pk of 20 percent.

AFTERMATH

"We have established air superiority over Iraq and can fly throughout the country with relative impunity."
Lt Gen Charles A. Horner, Commander of CENTAF, January 23, 1991

There can be little doubt that Operation *Desert Storm* was one of the most impressive military offensives in modern history, led – and enabled – in great part by the extensive, well-designed, and aggressively executed offensive air campaign. This nearly revolutionary aerial offensive was enabled by the victory of the five USAF F-15C Eagle fighter squadrons and their almost hermetical establishment of a permissive environment that allowed other Coalition air operations to be conducted without threat of interference by IrAF interceptors.

For their part, as the opposition, Gen Muzahim Sa'ub Hassan's fighter squadrons were instructed to mount "a limited defense" that would uphold the reputation of the IrAF as a viable military arm in the region, while preserving a "force in being" that could be used once the war was over and the Americans went home. The heavy losses (relative to the

IrAF MiG-25RBT, serial number 25105, captured in 2003 near Qadessiya AB. It is now at the National Museum of the USAF in Dayton, Ohio, minus its wings, which could not be found. (USAF)

few air defense sorties flown) during the first three days/nights of combat operations revealed that these were mutually exclusive goals – the lopsided attrition experience by IrAF interceptor and fighter units precluded maintaining a viable force if operations were continued.

Prior to the war the IrAF averaged 235 sorties per day – during the first week of combat (January 17–23) this number was reduced to 30–40 sorties each day. By the end of the first week only five main airfields remained operational, and Iraqi air defense radar activity was reduced to only 20 percent of pre-war levels. When 117 IrAF combat aircraft were destroyed in their HASs, 107 others were flown to Iran for "safekeeping," 11 of which were lost during the operation. While the "Foxbats" "stayed home," 11 "Floggers" (seven MLs, four BNs – one crashed in Iran – and one UB two-seater) evacuated to Iran.

With victory incomplete, the F-15C Eagle was needed to police the skies of northern and southern Iraq for the next 12 years following Operation *Desert Storm*. Here, a fully armed 33rd FW Eagle does just that in December 1991 – notice that it is carrying a then brand new AIM-120 AMRAAM beneath its right wing, this weapon having been designed to make up for the deficiencies of the Vietnam-legacy AIM-7 Sparrow – four of which are also carried by the jet. (USAF)

Consequently, there was no IrAF opposition to the Coalition ground campaign. The Iraqis did not fly a single sortie for the two weeks prior to the ground offensive, and none during the operation. As a direct result, the ground offensive was impressively decisive, liberating Kuwait and crippling (though not destroying) Saddam Hussein's Republican Guard forces in 100 hours of combat – Coalition casualties totalled 390 personnel killed and 776 wounded, against varying estimates of 3,500 to 40,000 Iraqi dead.

Quite obviously the F-15C Eagle – except for its AIM-7 missiles – its pilots, maintenance crews, and AWACS controllers had performed superbly, convincingly meeting the fighter's design goal of being able to beat "any present or projected Soviet-designed fighter." In the short, sharp air war over Iraq it had bested the MiG-25, as well as the modern and more advanced MiG-29 "Fulcrum."

While the Iraqis were disappointed in their MiG-29s (and even more so in the MiG-23), the MiG-25 upheld its reputation as being their premier fighter, in spite of its dated technology. The official IrAF "after action" report's "lessons learned and recommendations" specified that "aircraft dedicated to the air defense purposes should be equal or superior to combat aircraft of the attacking nations with regard to radar detection ranges, the [radar] tracking capability and weapons firing ranges. The MiG-25 aircraft enjoyed the above characteristics of attacking and downing a number of enemy combat aircraft despite the enemy's air superiority."

For the next 12 years, the USAF Eagles dominated the skies of Iraq, enforcing the UN mandated "no fly zones" (NFZ) in an effort to prevent Saddam Hussein from using the IrAF against Kurdish and Shi'a enclaves within the country. Occasionally, surviving IrAF "Foxbats" – gathered into No. 96 Sqn – flew incursions into the NFZs to demonstrate Saddam Hussein's defiance of the UN sanctions, and on one occasion shot down an armed USAF RQ-1 Predator reconnaissance drone near Baghdad. To end the 12-year stand-off, Operation *Iraqi Freedom* was launched in 2003, but this time the IrAF's eight "Foxbats" – even augmented by six surviving MiG-23MLs and nine older MiG-23MFs (No. 93 Sqn) – launched no sorties in defense of their nation. Consequently, the Eagle was not needed, and no F-15C units actively participated in the final campaign to excise Iraq as a rogue nation.

FURTHER READING

An enormous number of books and magazine articles have been written about the American, British, and other Coalition partners' operations in what, in the West, is termed the "Gulf War." But to tell the full story of the battle for air supremacy over Iraq in early 1991, both sides' perspectives must be addressed, and this requires access to sources knowledgeable about the enigmatic IrAF, its equipment, forces, doctrine, strategy, plans, and operations. Little was known in the West until 2003 when, after the conclusion of Operation *Iraqi Freedom*, the US acquired a large number of surviving IrAF documents, many of which were translated and disseminated – known as the "Harmony" collection – to interested US government agencies and contracted consultants.

Particularly significant was the IrAF's official "after action report," entitled "The Role of the Air Force and Air Defense in the Mother of All Battles," dated November 5, 1991. This and other "Harmony" documents have been used by American research centers – such as the Institute for Defense Analyses – and some more objective authors, such as Michael Knights, to shed light on the Iraqi perspective of air operations during Operation *Desert Storm*.

For further study, the following are recommended:

Atkinson, Rick, *Crusade – The Untold Story of the Persian Gulf War* (Houghton Mifflin Company, 1993)

Barron, John, *MiG Pilot – The Final Escape of Lt Belenko* (McGraw-Hill, 1979)

Brown, Craig, *Debrief – A Complete History of U.S. Aerial Engagements 1981 to the Present* (Schiffer Military History, 2007)

Davis, Richard G., *On Target: Organizing and Executing the Strategic Air Campaign Against Iraq* (Office of Air Force History, 2002)

Deur, John M., "Wall of Eagles – Aerial Engagements and Victories in Operation *Desert Storm*," an unpublished manuscript commissioned by the USAF Historical Research Agency for its Gulf War Air Power Survey, AFHRA document NA-399

Gordon, Michael R., and Gen Bernard E. Trainor, *The Generals' War – The Inside Story of the Conflict in the Gulf* (Little Brown & Co., 1995)

Gordon, Yefim, *MiG-25 "Foxbat" MiG-31 "Foxhound" – Russia's Defensive Front Line* (Aerofax Inc./Midland Counties Publications Ltd., 1997)

Gordon, Yefim, and Keith Dexter, *MiG-23/27 "Flogger" – Soviet Swing-Wing Fighter/Strike Aircraft* (Aerofax Inc./Midland Counties Publications Ltd., 2006)

Gordon, Yefim, and Dmitriy Komissarov, *Soviet and Russian Military Aircraft in the Middle East* (Hikoki Publications, Ltd., Manchester, UK, 2013)

Knights, Michael, *Cradle of Conflict – Iraq and the Birth of the Modern U.S. Military* (Naval Institute Press, 2005)

"The Role of the Air Force and Air Defense in the Mother of All Battles," the Iraqi Air Force and Air Defense Command November 5 1991 "after action report" from Operation *Desert Storm*, captured at the IrAF HQ in 2003, and translated as "A 1991 Dossier on the Role of the Iraqi Air Force in the Gulf War" by the US DOD-sponsored Conflict Records Research Center (CRRC Record Number SH-AADF-D-000-396).

Sadik, Brig Gen Ahmad, and Tom Cooper, *Iraqi Fighters 1953–2003* (Harpia Publishing LLC and Moran Publishing LLC, 2008)

Woods, Kevin M., *Um Al Ma'arik (Mother of All Battles) – Operational and Strategic Insights from an Iraqi Perspective – Volume 1* (Institute for Defense Analyses, 2008)

INDEX

References to illustrations are shown in **bold**.